Some people say there are as many as 100,000 Down and Outs in Britain . . . people for whom no social services exist in a form in which they can make use of them.

This book is a study of some of them, these people who have fallen through the safety net of the welfare state.

Many are involved in 'the treadmill' – they pass needlessly between sleeping rough, common lodging house, psychiatric hospital, senseless and needless visits to prison.

Many, like Edna in Sandford's film *Edna, The Inebriate Woman*, have a drink problem. Others have other problems . . .

Sandford passes from a consideration of them, to a consideration of other unfortunates, especially our unmarried mothers and those needlessly incarcerated in institutions, above all those who, like his *Cathy*, end up in Homes for the Homeless.

Down and Out in Britain

Revised Edition

Jeremy Sandford

NEW ENGLISH LIBRARY
TIMES MIRROR

ACKNOWLEDGEMENTS

I am grateful to the following for permission to reprint prose appearing in this book:

Allen & Unwin Ltd. for an extract from *Mother and Baby Homes* by Jill Nicholson.

Christian Action for two extracts, from *The Treadmill* by David Brandon and from a pamphlet by Leslie Tuft.

Hamish Hamilton Ltd. for an extract from *Men in Prison* by Tom Clayton (Copyright © 1970 by Tom Clayton).

Hutchinsons & Co. for an extract from *The Unknown Citizen* by Tony Parker.

Oliphants Ltd. for an extract from *I Know It Was the Place's Fault* by Des Wilson.

First published in 1971 by Peter Owen Ltd.
Copyright © Jeremy Sandford 1971

*

FIRST NEL REVISED PAPERBACK EDITION NOVEMBER 1972

*

NEL Books are published by
New English Library Limited from Barnard's Inn, Holborn London E.C.1.
Made and printed in Great Britain by Hunt Barnard Printing Ltd., Aylesbury, Bucks

45001280 8

Contents

About Jeremy Sandford

Jeremy Sandford grew up in Herefordshire. He was educated at Oxford and in a touring military band in Germany in which he held the position of first clarinet.

He is a sponsor of 'Shelter', 'The Simon Community', and a Governor of 'The Cyrenians'. He is also editor of 'Romano Drom', a newspaper provided as a service to Gypsies.

His hobbies are riding, music, exploring and getting to know British people.

His next assignment takes him on a trip round the third world to write about Britain's part in it, in a book called 'Armies of Peace'.

His work has won major prizes and awards, including the Italia Prize, the Critics' Award and The Writers' Guild 'Best Play' Award.

INTRODUCTION

Into The Bilges

I descended into the bilges of society. Wearing boots that gaped at the seams and an ancient great-coat, I allowed my beard to grow and my hair to become matted with dirt. I wanted to meet and talk with down and outs, dossers, tramps, the inhabitants of kiphouses, derries, Spikes.[1]

I wanted to see what life is like at the bottom, for those who have failed, those whom the Welfare State has failed to reach.

Often, when in these nether regions, I was struck by the fact that those whom I met had once been respectable and 'successful' people. And I sensed a feeling of deep insecurity, the deep fear that I too might all too soon end up, derelict, on Britain's skid-row.

From down in the abyss the Welfare State can look like a ladder of which the last few rungs are broken or missing.

I sometimes had the fancy that perhaps the rest of my life was only an illusion – that those things I prized, friends, children, a home, were just a dream from which I would awaken back to the reality of the narrow dosshouse dormitory – nothing else. Once, some years ago, I attempted a similar book, and abandoned it.

This time I carried through.

And after some weeks in this nether area, I decided that it wasn't enough to write only an account of Britain's skid-row. I

1 A kiphouse is a common lodging house – the lowest form of night time accommodation. There are still thousands of beds in these places in Britain. The kiphouse is also known as the dosshouse. A derry is a derelict house in which people are sleeping rough There are still thousands of people doing this each night in Britain.

A spike is a state or local authority reception centre where you can stay free if you are destitute.

A dosser is someone who sleeps rough or regularly uses a dosshouse.

A skipper (or kipper) is the act of sleeping rough or a place to do it.

decided to try to do more. To draw back and ask why people are there. Why, in this, one of the richest countries of the world, there needs to be such an abyss.

More statistics and more information are available than there were in previous times. There has been more thinking about social conditions. I felt it would be wrong to write a book solely of reportage. I wanted to try to point to some reason.

Why do people fail? I came to the conclusion that one reason is that our Welfare State, theoretically resting on an ideal of love, has not yet learned how to carry through this ideal in every respect.

R. D. Laing has written of the violence that, in human relationships, can masquerade as love. The way that individuals often do violence to each other under the impression or with the pretence that this is love.

Can it be that the Welfare State also indulges in this sort of relationship? That its friendly embrace can be a disguise for something more like the kiss of death?

The thousands of families which have been broken up in Homes for the Homeless are a good example of this. Families which in almost any other country in the world would have lived out their days in reasonable happiness. Our State breaks up these families because it can find no home for them. In many other countries Cathy would still be together with her husband and children, in penury, in a shack. A question of priorities. Love or housing.

Good housing is the only real answer, but even a shack would be better than what happened to Cathy.

There is something else that should be said here. As our society comes to hold out more alleged boons to the citizenry, it also becomes more complex. The special skills required to survive in it become more exacting. People who were able to be absorbed in the old and relatively unsophisticated extended family or village setup now find it much harder. The number of those who need special help becomes greater.

That there should henceforth be freedom from want. With this brave concept the Welfare State was founded. There are still too many areas where we have failed. Ours is a society in which it is still all too easy to fail. A society in which the State, while appearing to offer a helping hand to those who get in a mess, instead too often administers a sharp kick in the crutch.

This country, our country, so good and just in some ways, is also a violent country in which those who run the law courts, prisons and institutions do not always perform as well as they should those things which we pay them to do.

Those who fail we do not always help. Instead, we punish them.

Jeremy Sandford

PART ONE

Sleeping Rough, and Days and Nights in the Kiphouse . . .

They are there tonight and they will be there tomorrow night . . . the thousands of people who, when most of us are in our beds, are out there sleeping rough in derelict buildings, barns, hedgerows, under the sky; wrapped in newspapers, old sacks, old clothes.

And, beyond these thousands of people, there stretch other, greater thousands – those who spend their lives in a senseless solitary trek between common lodging house, spike, psychiatric hospital, and often prison . . .

Many of the settled population have little pity for these lone anonymous people. But to them I would say two things; *first*, there but for the grace of God go you . . . in the nether regions of Britain I have been amazed how many were once 'of high estate'. And *second*, if you will not pity them, just consider how much these people cost us in taxes; it costs a fortune to send them on their treck through a host of inapropriate social services and institutions.

I wanted to meet those people, to talk to them face to face; these people who I had tried to portray in *Edna the Inebriate Woman*; these people whom Cathy in my play was in grave danger of joining when, stripped of her family at the end of the play, she walked alone away from the railway station.

'It's me legs, see, it's me legs.' The old lady who sat beside me on a bench at Waterloo Station wore an ancient great-coat and a pork-pie hat, from beneath which she peered out with moist and luminous eyes. She smelt. Her hair was matted with dirt.

'Yes, it's me legs play me up,' she said. 'In the summer, in the summer things are much better. It's while we have all this cold, that's when me legs go numb. And see me hands, too. And legs go numb with an awful lot of pain. . . .

'Well, like today, there was a little bit of sun, I went and sat in

13

the sun in the park, and I felt a great improvement. As long as it don't get too hot. But it don't do that this time of year. Too much hot draws it. Worse than the other. But we'll be all right now. The doctor told me that, one day when I went to see him, when I said, "Well doctor, sometimes the sun draws them, sometimes it's the cold, draws me veins, you see."

'If I can get a warm glow on me legs then that's good. I get it from the fire, when we light it behind the derries, that's the derelict houses. But I can't stand too much of it. Can't stand too much heat or the cold.'

One a.m. on Waterloo Station. On the pew-like benches twenty or thirty decrepit men and women were trying to sleep. A couple of policemen appeared and the decrepit men and women, sighting them, with the alacrity of a flock of birds rose and shuffled or hobbled off out of the station. A few remained uncomfortably sleeping and were rudely awakened.

We left the station in a motley crew, tramps, layabouts, dossers, meths drinkers, vagrants, the inmates of lodging houses, former inmates of psychiatric hospitals or of prisons, myself and a nun.

'What do you think of the fact that there's men sleeping out every night in London on the park benches?' the nun that I had come with asked. 'I suppose we must say, "Well, that's how it is, and that's all".'

'No, I think it's a very sad and shocking thing.'

'Is this the first time you have seen the soup run at work?'

'Yes. And the first time, in Britain, that I've seen such poverty.'

We lurched on through the streets, at the mercy of the execrable driving of Sister James.

As we went down along some arches under the railway by Waterloo Station, I saw fifty ragged men, many of them drunk, shuffling after the van, shuffling to be first in the place for the soup.

The back of the van was opened and the nuns carried out a large tureen of soup and began to ladle it out into plastic cups.

Other nuns went round handing out wads of four or five slices of bread by hand. The men were extremely ragged and many of them had bloated, blotched, hairy, unhealthy complexions. All wore overcoats.

I noticed one or two beautiful but threadbare girls amongst them.

The dust rose in the light of the headlamps and beneath the arches some of the men sat down and gnawed, several with gap-toothed gums, at the bread.

Every now and again the nuns, pretty young girls that they were, would catch sight of an Irishman and there would be cries, 'Ah, he's from Ireland!' as they clustered round him. When they gave out the soup or bread they didn't at once withdraw their hands but would leave them a moment as if offering spiritual as well as material assistance.

We went back to outside the station to see whether anyone would like to come for soup. A short and pathetic little man sat on one of the benches, pointing to his knee, saying, 'Feel it, feel it, they run me down, the bastards, they caught me in the street and they run me down!'

He was very drunk.

He seemed to subside into a deep sleep.

Then with a start he suddenly awoke, and saw a nun standing before him and he cried, 'Oh, I'm an Irishman! I've sinned! Oh, Holy Sister, save me!' Then he hid his head in his hands and wept.

His fly buttons sprang open and he looked up at the nuns, saying 'Sorry! Sorry!' Then later. 'Here's money for you, here's money for you.'

A nun asked, 'Have you been to the hospital?'

He said, 'Yes. But they wouldn't have me. They dressed me knee but that's all they did. Then they threw me out again.'

'Have you anywhere to go tonight?'

'No, I've nowhere to go. There's nowhere for me. Nowhere that'll have me.'

And again the man buried his face in his hands.

At his invitation I felt his knees. One of them was far larger and hotter than the other.

Other men, friends of his, came up and said, 'It's all right Sister, we'll take him to the hospital. But they won't have us.'

Again the poor old man proffered money for the nuns.

'No, you hold on to your money, you hold on to it.'

Another man appeared to be upset when he was approached and told that there was hot soup waiting for him in an archway.

He said, 'I'll admit, I'm down, but I'm not that down yet. I don't need charity yet.'

The Sister said, 'I'm sorry, I didn't mean to offend you.'

The man said, 'No, you're right, I'm down. But I don't need charity yet.'

We returned to the railway arch. By now there were a good hundred men clustering round the van. One, completely drunk with a

15

great blubber lower lip sticking out towards us staggered up to the van. 'Soup, soup, I've only just arrived!'

'But that man's had four cups already!'

'Soup! Soup!' Now the man's face was practically in the van. 'Aw fuck! Fuck!' he cried, and worse.

Now he had got the door open and was climbing in after the nuns.

'Quick, give the man the soup!' said the Mother Superior.

Our next stop was the Embankment Gardens by Temple Station.

A priest who was travelling with us went ahead to see if there was anybody there. 'Yes, there's lots and lots,' he cried, coming back to the van. So the nuns climbed out with their tureens of soup and went down into the middle of the gardens where I counted twenty-five men, most of them apparently asleep in spite of the frost, asleep under their great-coats, some of them under newspapers, one of them under a long roll of brown paper wound round him again and again. These men didn't leave their seats. If they did, they might forfeit them. The nuns went round patting them in turn on the shoulder and asking them, 'Good evening, would you care for some soup, sir?' Many of them muttered confusedly or asked the nuns to go away, but before long, most of them had woken up and were drinking their soup.

In the nineteenth century General Booth rode over Vauxhall Bridge and was horrified to find men sleeping out in the open to the South of the river. This was one of the things that led him to found the Salvation Army.

Now he would not need to cross the river to see them.

The thirty men sleeping in the Embankment Gardens were more silent than those I saw under the arches at Waterloo Station. Only one stumbling figure emerged from the dusk, shambled up to the tureen, asked for soup, and then wandered off again, back into the night.

The others, lounged along their seats on this freezing night, sipped their soup and then settled back to sleep. All too soon the police would come and move them on.

One man had the trembles and he spilt not one but three cups of soup before he was able to drink it. The soup splashed all over him as if he'd been sick. He spilt it too all over the habit of a nun, and then vomited. But the nun still held out her hand, in mercy, as the soup trickled over it.

We continued along the streets by the Savoy Hotel.

It was past midnight but they were still filled with people, cars like costly jewels, smoothly dressed men and their lovely girl-friends.

The Mother Superior said, 'Oh, you see all types at this time of night in London. You see all sides of life.'

We turned up a back street by the Strand Palace Hotel, and this was the most macabre place that we visited, for here there were two vast windows, meshed across the front not with glass but with wire netting. And against this there clung twenty or twenty-five men, gaunt silhouettes against the background of light, clinging on with grubby fingers, pressed against the wire netting, trying to pick up a touch of that warmth. As the van drew up they shifted a little and fighting broke out between two of them, each trying to oust the other from his place at the window. I remember a tall, amazing looking man with mongoloid features, a veritable giant, standing in the best place of all, in the centre of one of the windows. These men spoke little as the nuns went amongst them with their cups of soup.

A girl in a fur coat, taking a short cut home, gave this crowd of silent, derelict people a wide berth.

A conventionally dressed man, like a clerk, was drinking the soup avidly. 'I was intended for the medical profession. But I was inadequate. I was in the army and while I was there I saw a lot of pain, a lot of suffering. The cries that men made when they were dying, the sounds they produced, these were incredible. I didn't start drinking then, but when I got back to civilian life I didn't seem able to cope with it and I started drinking.

'I am inadequate. I must be. I must be inadequate to just drink all my money. I go on a milk round, they pick me up every morning at five, up there. I get quite good money, but I drink it all. I drink so much I don't even have any left for my bed. And so I sleep out, standing.'

An old, plump, pleasant looking lady approached.

'Ah yes, they're such nice looking young men, such nice look-ing boys,' she exclaimed. 'You wouldn't think they had the devil in them but they do.'

She turned on me, 'And there's another! There's another one, he's been round me too, and taking my purse and going through all my papers and all me other things, they took me knife and fork, they look all right but the devil's in them. Look at him, isn't he smart!'

'Sure he's an Irish boy,' said the nun.

'He may be an Irishman, yet he's full of the devil. The devil is very strong, the devil is everywhere.'

'Yes, but God is there too to give us strength,' said the nun. 'He's there to give us a helping hand.' And she stretched out her own hands in a rather beautiful gesture towards the derelict man.

'No, he does not have God in him, he has the devil in him.'

'Well,' said the young man, 'I try to give a bit of trade to both parties.'*

I returned to outside Waterloo Station and talked to a woman.

'Does your mind get cloudy?' she asked me. 'My mind gets cloudy. There's times I've tramped all night and I've kept on after the day has broken. And I've kept on tramping and I've been going through a little town. People are getting up, the cafs are beginning to open, and you can smell the breakfasts being cooked. And you haven't got any money to buy your breakfast yourself, all you can afford is a drink from the village pump, a drink of water. And you can't stop because the police will move you on. And it's pointless to stop. You've got to keep going so you say, All right, I'll go on to Keswick. So you got a target, you go to Keswick. And when you get to Keswick you say, I'll go on to Aberdeen. And from there. . . . '

Through the narrow streets, across an old bombsite, under some ruined tottering buildings, and now I stumble over filthy earth and a mass of tattered masonry till on the farther side I reach a building.

It's derelict. Toothless windows gape. Inside, a fire is burning and ten hunched great-coated figures sit round it.

'I can't get a decent place. It's because I've got no lolly.

'And I can't get no lolly because I'm dirty, the vermin is crawling all over me.

'And I'm dirty because I ain't got no washing place in a decent place to live.

'And I ain't got no decent place to live because I ain't got no lolly. And I ain't got no lolly because I'm dirty.'

From a member of the Simon Community Trust,* I learned details of other dossers.

'This fellow, he hanged himself in the nick. He said there was nothing for him to look forward to when he came out. So, when it got to the time that he was due for his release, he hung himself. He reckoned prison was as close to a real home as he'd ever get.'

'Well, I haven't had a bath for, well, now, for months. I know I stink. I know I'm loused up. Well, I'm a little timid, that's why. I

*Asterisks indicate more information in the notes at the end of the book.

know I could go to the Spike (Reception Centre). But I can't stick that inspection and the way they treat you there. And I can't get the social security because I haven't got a fixed address.* They say, why don't you go to the Spike. But I can't stand it at the Spike.

'And I can't get clothes no more from the charity because I had too many from them in the past. What I wanted from life was a happy family life like. But I never got it. My Mum and Dad they parted so I was brought up by me Aunt. And that's what I do now. Half the time down on the benches, down by the sea, then I come up to London, hitch a lift on a lorry, and then I live up here in the derries.

'I go for the scrumpy, you know, that cheap rough cider. I'm fairly hooked on that. I go on the social security, for about ten bob a day you can be drunk most of the day. But then they wouldn't pay me no more, and cider got too expensive for me so then I went on the meths and I've been having metal polish. Metal polish in a sandwich. What do you want, if I went to hospital I'd have to dry out there, and that would be worse than staying like I am. So I just go and have another drink in the tombyard.

'As I see it, life's like a pole, a slippery pole. It's easy to slide down but it's hard ever to slide up again. Once you're down, then you never get up no more. Sometimes I think about the future. What's there in the future? Nothing.'

Another man spoke of the time when he made good money, mining uranium in Canada. He went there after a youth spent largely in Approved School, Borstal and prisons. He came back to England with a few hundred pounds, and blued it all in a couple of months. After that, Waterloo Station.

In the churchyard, old sodden paper parcels and cardboard packets lie beneath the trees, and empty bottles of V.P. wine and methylated spirits.

A large wooden notice says: 'Wanted, Discarded Clothing for our Homeless Men. SUITS. OVERCOATS. SOCKS. SHOES. Winter's coming.'

Two pork chops, mouldy, lie unexpectedly underneath the trees, and a sodden bit of newspaper saying, 'Shots in London. Near Miss Drama'. Another notice tells me that organ and piano music can be heard in the church on Tuesday.

I join a crowd of one hundred and fifty frayed men waiting in the churchyard. Some sit on wooden seats. Behind them are the tombs. One of the benches has a large charred gap where it must have caught fire (perhaps as a result of some misunderstanding). There are four dustbins, filled with old shoes and overcoats.

More empty bottles of V.P. wine lie on the ground, sodden paper cups, and a bottle of Surgical Meths and another empty bottle of Mineralised Meths in a tin, proclaiming: 'Not to be taken. Keep out of reach of children.'

I stand amongst the waiting men in a strange atmosphere of peace, as far away a police car passes, headlamps on, siren blasting, flashing by in the street outside the churchyard.

This is St Botolph's Church in Aldgate, originally just outside the Eastern gates to London. St Botolph was the patron saint of travellers. One of the men here is on crutches. Many of them walk at unusual angles, or have unusual physical characteristics. Filth, filth, everywhere.

A paper notice on the door informs us that the crypt is open from 6 p.m. to 9 a.m. and that services available include distribution of clothes (on Monday), haircuts (on Tuesday), clothes, washing facilities, provision of shoe laces and buttons, first aid, and playing cards.

The crypt will not be open for a while, so I take a walk round the area. Shops emerging from tangles of corrugated iron, kosher butchers. A girl runs out ahead of me like a partridge that has been flushed, a little powder lightly sprayed round her eyes. She rushes down a back alley and disappears through a door. A stout procurer with long black colpons of ugly hair says to me, 'Can I help you ducks?'

I reach another church, built by Hawksmoor, whose front has been hidden by huge railings on which hangs a notice: 'Not intended to deny access to the church but to prevent improper use of the porch'. I look up at the noble fabric and see where one window has broken and a cat is peering out. Then I return to the crypt. Men pushing now to try to get in. Entry is being made hard by an old man who lies completely drunk across the entrance in his battered great-coat.

Muscular Christianity here assumes a new meaning, for the vicar, in grey flannel shirt sleeves, is trying bodily to drag him away, drag him out of the door, so the others can get in.

'Don't you fuckin' fuckin' move me! Fuckin' leave me alone!' The dossers are crowding round the top of the alleyway leading down to the crypt, enjoying the spectacle. The man on crutches staggers up to me and murmurs something fast and unintelligible.

Meanwhile, sitting on the occasional seat, other great-coated groups of dossers watch with appreciation the hurly-burly going on. The vicar dislodges the drunk and he staggers out. A half empty bottle of wine falls out from his coat and the other dossers applaud. 'Well, this is not a pub,' says an old boy sagely. 'You can't bring drink in here, treat it like a pub!'

Winding through the vaults of this old crypt, the men have made a long ragged queue. And, seeing this grimy scene, I think to myself: This is the way things should be – not only for down and outs, but, perhaps, for all of us. A fatherly crypt where all will be welcome. Maybe pubs were once like this.

The queue slowly, infinitely slowly, moves forward, and at a counter nicely spoken women and men hand out tin mugs of tea and slices of bread and butter. The walls and ceiling of the crypt are painted cream and brown. Copper tubing has been painted over but shines out brightly where the shoulders and coats of dossers have rubbed against it. With their mugs of tea and bread, the men sit down on long benches.

I notice that the queue never gets shorter. When dossers have finished their tea and slices, they squeeze up and join on again, pretending they've just arrived. I don't suppose the management minds.

I settle down with my mug in one of the crowded vaults.

There is a woman playing cards, who never stops talking, and she has a speech impediment which makes her voice a bit strident. 'Well, I told him. I told him I'd see him when he come out of hospital and this morning he come out of hospital but he ain't come to see me yet, I'm worried because I'm in work now ain't I, I just got in work this morning, I went to work for the first time this morning, so I can't hang around here in the churchyard all day waiting for him to turn up now can I?'

A battered man with wayward charm comes and sits down beside her. 'Hullo darling,' he says drunkenly, 'now tell me who's the most handsome man in the room and why am I?' Suddenly he is assaulting her, feeling her all over, but members of the staff cause him to desist. Nearby a scholarly looking man is scribbling in a notebook. A man in the usual dosser's outfit of great-coat, boots, his legs covered with sores, leans over to me, 'It's no good tonight, there's too many here. One hundred, that's about when it's nice. But when you get all this lot, there's lots come over from Cable Street, that's too much anyway, you're not meant to come every night are you, I'm not coming back here not till Thursday. I'll stay at the Middlesex Sally Anne actually, it's all right there, but they started praying more than they used to and I don't like that. I'm not keen on religion.'

The man with the wayward charm says, 'Well, I'm a nice man, sit all on me own, I'm a nice man. I just sits there don't say anything, drinks me tea.'

I ask him what are his plans for tonight.

'Well, I'm going to sit here and drink my tea then I'm going to go back to the Salvation Army and watch the Telly, and then I'm going to beddy beddy, beddy-byes.'

'Where've you been today?' one dosser asks his neighbour.

'Walking around the city. Where've you been?'

'I went to Chiswick to see a mate of mine. Once gave me breakfast but this time he wouldn't. He's got some discs there, I saw them. He didn't want to know me. I've got a good mind to go back and nick them.'

'Where Irish eyes are smiling,' sings another man.

A couple more of the servers arrive. There is a great cooing of 'Hul*lo*!' and 'How *are* you', from behind the bar.

Talking, toffee-nosed, one of the dossers says, 'Oh yes, actually I'm staying in the Hotel, the Hotel in South London, I hexpect you know the one I mean, the Spike.'

And, thinking of hotels, I think to myself that the very poor in Britain are in some ways rather like the very rich. They constitute Britain's leisured classes. The rich man doesn't have to work and can choose which hotel to stay in. So can the dosser. Both have the problem of shortage of beds, of having to book in advance. They use the same country, but different maps.

Dossers have quite a wide choice of hostels. They talk knowledgeably about them, 'Oh yes, well, St Crispin's, it's just a night's shelter, it's not a proper hostel.' 'Give me Great Peter Street any day.' 'Going to do a skipper tonight. I feel like sleeping out.'

These tortuous winding vaults feel rather like an air-raid shelter. Down here it seems as if we are sitting out some catastrophe which threatens us all. The vaults are like one of those exotic rooms in which, threatened by the plague, people whiled away their last days of life. I feel a great compulsion myself to give in, to let go. What's the point of hanging on to these threadbare status-giving trappings of our empty and callous civilisation.

Those who are here clearly feel the same. Every now and again one of those sitting at the long benches succumbs to the enemy. With an eerie hoot he falls down on the floor, or bursts into raucous song, or forgetfully assaults one of the staff.

The vicar is dealing with one such man now. 'Either you behave yourself or out you go!' he shouts.

Not far away a group of boys are sitting round with their feet immersed in bowls of boiling water, caressed by steam. The look on their faces is blissful.

I peer into farther catacombs, all filled with this same anonymous vociferous yet silent crowd of great-coated men.

One of the staff of a similar place said, 'Most of them have got apart from their homes. They have nobody to care for them and nobody for whom to care.

'It may be that a wife has died and they've never got over it. It may be that a wife has walked out on them, and then of course the question is, why did she walk out? What happened in that sad instance? Or something else.

'And so we get them trying to win forgetfulness for a time, either through beer, or, more common now, through methylated spirits or surgical spirits. You can get a bottle of methylated spirit for two shillings in the chemist's, and half of that takes you out of Aldgate and East London very quickly.

'Sometimes I invite them to dinner in my home and then they will spruce themselves up, get a bit of a wash, and a shave; they come into our sitting room, and really try to make the most of the evening.

'The other week, going home in my car, one of them said to me, "You know, I haven't been in a house for over three years. I've been in the nick (you know, that's prison) and I've been in the Sally Anne (that's the Salvation Army Hostel) but I haven't been in a home for over three years."

'Well now, it's pretty awful to be in that state.

'He had cut down on his drink for that evening, and all the time when he wasn't eating, he was talking. When he was in his better self he told me that he really did want to get right. He started life in New York, in a very poor family. His mother had nine children, his father was a drunk, and never really brought home his wages. And he said, "I was the eldest. And the only thing that helped my mother was for me to go out and flog food, or vegetables, for money, or anything that I could flog. I don't think it was wrong, do you?" And I had to reply, "No, I think society was wrong in not coming to your help."

'But of course, unfortunately, we are often let down by these friends of ours. With a bit of effort and a lot of friendship some of them will go without a drink for a fortnight. Then comes the sudden failure, and the bout of hard drinking.

'Now, my own understanding of this is, not to blow them up, not to make them feel even more of a failure for letting us down, but to say, "You've done a damn good job in going sober and

23

straight for a fortnight. Now next time let's hope it's three weeks."

'I think I'm beginning to understand what goes on in their minds. They are not sure whether we're really sincere. Whether we can stand anything. And so they will try one thing after another, until they see that nothing they can do can really stop our friendship.'

A friend working in a Mission to down and outs gave me suitable clothes.*

He gave me heavy and filthy boots, tied with string. He gave me shapeless hideous trousers, and the sort of shirt that has no collar.

He gave me a succession of other tattered shirts to wear under this, and string to go round my trousers below the knee to keep out the cold.

He helped me to wrap newspaper round myself above the lowest layer of clothing but below the next, explaining that this would serve as an insulation through the nights. He gave me a hole-filled cap.

Finally, and most important, he gave me a vast and amorphous great-coat, and told me to fill its pockets with odds and ends and wear it at all times, even when it was hot.

To complete the disguise I let my beard go long, and didn't wash my hands so that, soon, dirt congregated under my nails.

A street of derelict houses. My companion put a shoulder against the decrepit door. It rasped open and in a moment we were clanking across corrugated iron lying on the floor in the darkness.

Through a doorway to my right I saw the guttering flames of a fire and a number of young people lying on the floor.

'Don't go in there – just a load of hippies,' said my guide.

Beneath my feet I saw where the floor yawned away giving a glimpse of more flames, guttering far beneath me.

'Careful, there's a step missing there.'

We stumped down the staircase and at the bottom I found, huddled by the light of a candle and the dancing flames, grimed, seamy, basic people, the sort that Rowlandson painted.

'See that one over there? The one with his shirt open to his waist? That's Irish Mick. He's one of the most famous characters around here.'

'Who's this? The law?' asked Irish Mick, looking glitteringly in my direction.

'No, he's all right.'

'He looks like the law to me.'

Irish Mick was holding a saucepan close to the brick wall where water was drizzling down. When the saucepan was full he moved it over to the fire where some banisters were burning.

'What d'you people live on?' I asked. 'Do you go to the social security?'

'No! No! Not bloody likely! Go there, they'll lock you up. I'll tell you. Many been in the nick. And there's the rest been in the mental places.'

My eye rested a moment on a man sitting in the corner, jerking his head back and forth in a bird-like movement. He wore baggy, dirty, grey flannels, boots, collar, a sports jacket, but with no shirt beneath it.

'And as to the social security, well they don't give you nothing till you got a fixed address, do they?'

I knew that this was no longer officially so, and I was interested when he elaborated, 'They give you a chit to the lodging house if you ask them, which lets you be there a week. But that's not helping a man. That's not helping him no ways. That's just pushing him down farther. That's not helping him to get up, pushing him down even farther from where he come from.

'No, we lives on the vegetables. The vegetables we get from the market after it's closed, you know, the ones they leave in the street they say is no good. We make a good stew from them.'

'Irish Mick says he's God. Tell 'em how you realised you was God.'

Irish Mick said, 'Oh well, I was praying one night. Then I realised I was praying to myself. There was no one there. So I knew I must be God.'

Some hippies came down and joined us. They were passing an inhaler between them. 'You're meant to sniff at it, it clears your nose. But if you break it and stuff the whole lot up, it sends you high. It's crazy. It makes you see the most crazy things.' They sat round in a circle snuffing at the capsule, shaking backwards and forwards in simulated giggles. An old man, sleeping beneath piles of newspapers in the corner, woke up and regarded the group of wheezing, gesticulating hippies with amazement.

Back in the street I noticed Edna, a little old lady in a great-coat, pass by. In her hand she held a black polythene bag, containing what, I wondered.

I was learning to recognize the sort of person about whom I wanted to know more. I followed her. A pork-pie hat was stuffed down over her head and her skirts were so long that they almost

25

rubbed the ground leaving little room to see beneath them her grubby stockings. She was trailing along the street being constantly overtaken by those who walked faster than her. At one point she was considerably confused. Her usual afternoon beat had evidently been blocked by building operations. She had to make a lengthy detour, then went to the outside snack bar that she always used at this time in the afternoon, and bought a pennyworth cup of tea which she munched with heavy toothless movements of her jaws, glancing at the girls in their mini-skirts as they pranced by. Then she continued along the dusty street.

Nearby, through large windows, in the centrally heated restroom of a publicity agency, she could see men sitting around with their feet up, asleep. But she passed them by. This figure who might belong to either sex seemed totally solitary and alone.

Now she wandered off again. A notice said, 'Can the Westminster Marriage Bureau help you? Yes, why not? Why not pop in and ask?'

But even as she gazed through the panes a man was dismantling the frayed curtains and tatty notices. She went down into the public conveniences, and whereas other countries have designed mosaics or at any rate inspiring texts for their public places, the British State does not seem to have been particularly imaginative in this direction.

'The consumption of alcohol and drug taking in public conveniences have led to serious acts of misconduct', said one of the notices. 'The convenience attendant will call the police immediately any breach of the Corporation's by-laws occurs.'

Another notice said, 'Loitering is prohibited. Beware of pickpockets'.

She was scrubbing away at her hands now, trying to get them clean at the rinsing basin of the public conveniences. Another notice addressed her, 'V.D. is nearly always caught by having sex with an infected person.'

She climbed up to street level again. And across the street the multi-storeyed eminence of the St Ermin's Hotel rose. A revolving triangle with silver letters advertised, 'New Scotland Yard'.

Now I was sitting on a little patch of grass in the centre of a roundabout. As the traffic went streaming by, a crowd of down and outs were sitting in decrepit clothes surveying the world.

'Oh yes,' said the old lady, 'that happened many a time. But in these days I never talk. Never talk to nobody, not to a soul. Because, I very rarely have anything to say or anyone to talk to. I didn't mix with anyone then and I don't mix with nobody now dear, nobody, not a soul. I'm on the road, that's it, and I don't need any to talk to.'

Outside a Hostel. A number of frayed people waiting. A notice saying, NO BEDS. A man stepped gently up to me. He had a long, bird-like, dry skull of a face with piercing blue eyes, and asked me if there were any beds going.

'I don't know. What's it like in there?'

He looked at me with his great sad composure. 'It's cold, man, cold.'

The side of his mouth twisted for a moment into a grin. 'You'd be better off under a bus, man, or under a tree. By the way, you know of anyone care to publish some drawings? I was a commercial artist once. I had a portfolio once.'

'Have you still got it?'

'No. Somebody whipped it.'

I asked him, 'Will they take you in here without money?'

Again the momentary wry grin. Then he looked at me a long sad time from his piercing eyes.

'How would they take you in without money?' he said gently, as if speaking of a miracle.

A young Irishman with a pleasant, friendly, sad face joined us.

'Any beds, guv?'

'No beds.'

'Any chance if you queue?'

'Well I queued last night, I queued two hours, but then at the end of it all there was nothing.'

The man sloped off, dignified, sad. The Irishman said, 'No, there's many things pull a man down. That man we were talking to, he comes of better stock than me, but now he's down. Sometimes it's the nerves. Sometimes it's family troubles. Sometimes they get to be worrying about things.'

'Where's the best derries?'

'Farther along the road, mate, the road to nowhere. I'm under psychiatric treatment actually.'

I found myself disliking intensely something about this man, irrationally. From his trousers he got out a grubby card which he presented to me. It told me the name of a well-known mental hospital. Then he said, 'Does your mind get far away sometimes? All far away? I go round the doctors. I get the various different drugs and help. I'm sick you see, sick. There's many people take an interest in me but it don't help. I let them down, you see. One tip I will give you. You got a wife? Yes, well hold on to her. Once

27

you lose them you won't get them back. Make a note of this. Phanyl. Write that down. Phanyl. P-H-A-N-Y-L. It's a good drug. Good for women.

'My mind gets so far away sometimes I walk all the way to Oxford to cure it. It takes me just all one night. When I get there I feel so fed up, that I turn round and walk back to London.'

'Where can we get a cup of tea?' I asked.

The man took me down the street to a mean little cafe, narrow like a passage, swept by draughts, lit by huge windows where dossers were dipping pieces of bread into Bovril. The jukebox sang: 'Last night as I lay sleeping I dreamed I was in your arms. ...'

'Why do I do it?' said an old white-haired dosser whom I found rummaging through a dustbin. 'I don't know. I've been on the road for thirty years now, but I still don't know why I do it. It's not good. To lay in all day and all night drinking, sicking up and vomiting and then drinking again. Here, you have some.'

He handed me a bottle and I drank a rapid gulp. The taste was totally disgusting. Quick! Quick! He was handing me a Polomint. 'Swallow that, that makes it good.' I sucked at the Polomint and it did just make tolerable the bitter rasping fire of the methylated spirits. He was laughing gaily.

But I knew that later the sickness would hit him.

'Now come on, drop that bloody bomb afore winter come', read the pencil scrawl on the wall of the ablutions.

I stood in half an inch of putrid water. Piles of sodden newspapers rotted into the floor or stuck in little mountains onto the corrugated iron walls. Beside the thirty-fifth bowl was an empty bottle of surgical spirit. Plugless, the dirty basins stretched away in rows. The essence of dosshouse life. The essence of despair.

The inmates of this tragic place crowded round me. A man with a strap in place of his right arm was trying to shave with his left hand with just a razor blade.

Places like this house up to a thousand men; mainly (though of course not always) they are the failures of our time, those who have fallen through the net of affluence that we've created, the alchos, the junkies, the winos, the bums, the ex-recidivists, the ex-mental hospital inmates, those maimed in body or mind. The halls and dormitories of the dosshouse are the ultimate stop for people like you and me should we hit bad luck and find ourselves slipping down Britain's skid-row.

There are hundreds of dosshouses in Britain. They house between them tens of thousands of Britain's 'forgotten men'.

In the 'recreation rooms' of these dosshouses, I have met an ex-lawyer, a former pressman, N.C.O's, an ex-schoolmaster, a ship's captain, council employees.

I visited an imposing building whose broken windows had been patched up with newspaper and old pillows. Inside, for floor after floor, there stretched a warren of little stalls, most of them without any direct access to the outside air, measuring six feet by three, and topped by wire-mesh netting to prevent thieving.

The cells contained nothing but a mean bed (with a horse-hair mattress) and a locker. Each bed had two or three threadbare blankets and sheets made from old sacks, some stamped, 'St Laurence High Ratio Flour'. There was choking dust everywhere. In one of the lockers I found a milk bottle filled with urine. I counted three hundred little cells in this place.

Glasgow has one of the worst down and out problems in Britain. I was there when one hundred dossers assembled in the Tent Hall Mission, just off the Saltmarket, at 8 a.m. on a Sunday morning, for mugs of tea and packages containing pies, hymns and a sermon.

On Sunday evening at the Lodging House Mission, East Campbell Street, near Glasgow Cross, one hundred and forty men and forty women dossers assembled for hunks of bread and tin mugs of tea, more hymns and another sermon.

The Chaplain said this, 'We have a service on Sunday evenings when we give them a big cup of tea and sing hymns, and hold services in some of the lodging houses. In addition we have soup kitchens twice a week, and a clothing store from which we hand out ten thousand articles of clothing a year.

'These men really do seem to have hit rock bottom, and what is tragic about them is that their numbers seem to be increasing, particularly among the younger men.

'The other day a distinguished but rather sad looking man came in to see me. During the interview I learned that he was once a well-known variety artist, unemployed since the advent of T.V. made the variety theatres close.

'We were able to give him a meal of two boiled eggs, bread and butter, and some fresh fruit. He spoke five languages and had travelled all over the world entertaining in some of the best hotels.'

As I left, an ancient woman dosser staggered up asking for clothes. Although it was November, she wore neither shoes nor stockings over her filthy legs and feet.

At another Glasgow dosshouse you have to leave 3d deposit for each knife, fork, or spoon. When I went the floor was littered with newspaper, and most of the hundred men sitting there who were actually eating were doing so with their fingers, not having been able to afford the deposit.

In many of these dosshouses the sheets are changed once a week, no matter how many people may have slept in them. Often there are few amenities, no towels, no lavatory paper, no plugs to the basins, no lavatory seats or locks to the toilet doors.

Many dosshouses have a proliferation of notices that might (or might not) make you feel at home; for instance, 'Do Not Raise Your Voices. Remember that these washrooms lie directly beneath the Officers' quarters.' A notice inside the main entrance to one hostel I visited said, 'Anyone wetting their bed will be barred from future entrance'.

The kiphouses of Britain don't advertise. Often there is no name over their doorways. You can often recognise them, though, by the collection of aimless and frayed men standing outside.

Down a short passage, and you enter a typical 'recreation room'. It has a concrete floor, the low ceiling held up with iron pillars, and at forty or fifty tables sit a few hundred men. As I look round I notice how many of the dossers sit at separate tables, ignoring one another, staring into space. Some are peering at single pieces of newspaper. Every half-hour a cry goes up, the doors leading up to the dormitories are flung open, and those who are tired of being awake take their places in the queue to stagger up to bed.

Bert Merryweather was a good-looking young man, easy-going, a little simple, but he was doing all right. As a young boy he'd been in an orphanage, and then he'd been in the army, and after that he'd got a job as a farm labourer, and he was happy doing this. Once he set out to find his mother, someone had given him an address that they said was his mother's, but when he arrived he found she wasn't there.

He was a good labourer, down on the farm in Devon, he was a cowman and he was a good cowman, some people said he was a little simple, why did he never marry, why didn't he go out in the evening. But his employer said, 'He's all right. He's splendid with the cows. He may be a little simple, but he's got a kind heart.'

And Bert carried on for twenty years at that farm, living and eating with his employer's family, and he was happy there.

One day he came in from milking with a pain in his chest. His employer said that he must go to the doctor about it. He did, and the doctor said it was the damp that was doing it. Bert must find another job.

So Bert looked, and he tried various jobs; he was a waiter, he washed up, but he was unable to stay in any of them. Somehow he didn't seem able to adapt. So, against his own better judgement, his employer took him back. He worked on the farm for another two years, and then became seriously ill.

When he left hospital the doctor told him, 'There's one thing you must promise; never go back to the farm'.

So, for the first time in his life, Bert came up to London, because here, he'd been told, there were jobs to be had. He hitch-hiked, and when the man giving him a lift told him they'd reached London, he jumped down and asked for the nearest Labour Exchange. He asked if they had got any jobs. But the man was busy, it was twelve o'clock on a Saturday morning, he was told, 'We can't see you now, come back on Monday morning.'

Bert said, 'The thing is I haven't brought much money with me.'

'Well, go to the national assistance.'

He went to the national assistance, but it was closed.

Bert was not a sophisticated person, but even if he had been it's difficult to see what he could have done.

He spent the weekend sleeping in a park, and on Monday morning, when he was due to return, he caught sight of his reflection in a pond where he'd gone to have a drink of water.

He hadn't shaved, and his whole face and body were plastered in mud from where he'd been sleeping.

He thought to himself, 'I can't go to the national assistance looking like this.'

He stayed at large for two days more, caught in a vicious circle, without the money to smarten himself up, and without the courage to go to the national assistance looking as he did.

The fifth day, famished with hunger, he nicked a milk-bottle off a doorstep. And a squad-car happened to be watching him. He was sent to prison.

He didn't go to prison for very long, but when he came out he was even more ashamed of himself, even less anxious to appeal for help.

A prisoners' charity gave him a pound and a letter to the national assistance.

The national assistance gave him a chit entitling him to a lodging in a dosshouse.

And there he remained.

You might say that any man in his senses would have got himself out of this situation. But the point is that there are a lot of people around who find it hard to do what other people find easy. A man like Bert is someone who finds it difficult to survive in a complicated society like ours. To give him a chit to a dosshouse is kicking a dog when it's down.

A drunk staggers up to me, 'I'll give you a little advice. Go down the Spike. They'll start you off. They've got this scheme. Say you want to go into catering. They'll look after you. Like, you know, dish scrapin', pot cleaning-uppin', they'll start you off.'

'Did you do that?'

'Yeah, I did that. But I didn't stick it. No, I couldn't stick it.'

Years ago, many of them would have been 'vagrom men', travelling from farm to farm after the seasonal crops ('hay in August, hops in September, apples in October, beets in November, starve, Lord save us, at sodding Christmas').

Farms are mechanised now, and casual wards are closing. It is the big cities that offer the casual work, so that our down and out population has become largely static. 'Instead of moving them on, now, we settle them down.'

The streets and roads of Britain have always been full of a certain number of wandering men and women, especially in times of unemployment. Another type of person who contributed to this were Navvies, the abbreviated name for the navigators, those who came over in the eighteenth century to build our canals, navigating their way through the countryside, and then turned their attention to the railways and later to the roads.

Talking to down and outs is nearly always moving. In so many ways they follow the Christian tenets on which our society is supposed to be based better than us, the 'successful' ones.

They really do take no thought for the morrow. They don't seek to lay up worldly goods, they are truly meek and indeed again and again turn the other cheek to a society which seems almost to enjoy hitting them.

'The staff have respect for a man if he's over twelve stone,' I was told.

An old dosser told me that, given the choice, he'd rather spend the rest of his life in prison than in a lodging house. 'The food's better, the beds aren't loused up, you have to sacrifice your freedom, it's true, but then you've got security. You know you can't be thrown out, at any rate till your time is up.'

The Rev. Ian Henderson, a founder of the Christian Action Hostels for Homeless Women,* tells me, 'The dosser's world is getting smaller. In May 1968 the official Ministry of Social Security Reception Centre at Western Road, Birmingham, was closed. A new place was opened, ten miles out, at Lye in Worcestershire. Applicants for admission have to apply for vouchers during daylight hours at the local offices of the Department of Health and Social Security. And, during the hours of darkness, at Digbeth Police Station.

'But the down-and-out mentality is one that is terrified of all forms of officialdom, above all that of the local police. The fact that most vagrants are deeply suspicious of all authority seems to have escaped the planners who devised the new arrangements.'

Another man tells me, 'With the slow but steady orientation of our society away from a working-class culture and towards a bourgeois culture with all its concepts of cleanliness, fitted carpets, decency and the rest, there no longer exist the faded thieves' kitchens catering for those who want to live at a lower social level. Those boarding houses described by George Orwell, where a rope is hung across the wall and the men lean across it, sleeping, and in the morning it is dropped and the men fall on the floor, would have suited these men very well.

'Nothing at this level of hygiene exists any more, possibly because the local authorities, all hot and idealistic with their latest plans to stamp out verminous and insanitary conditions, would close them down.

'So, at the standard of living which they have chosen, there is little for them, apart from the derries or the public parks and urinals.

'If they present themselves at hospital, they may get treatment for some specific ailment, but will not be allowed to stay very long and anyway, the nurses will very likely refuse to look after a man who is verminous, unwashed and perhaps abusive and half dead with alcohol.

'If they go to a psychiatric hospital they may only be allowed to stay for a certain time, in that the problem may not be that they have a disturbed mind, but merely that the conditions of life outside, for someone who wants to live as they do, are intolerable.

'People are still frequently leaving mental hospital without anywhere to go. This need not reflect badly on the social workers connected with the hospitals. Often patients discharge themselves or even escape. And others, when asked by the social worker where they will go when they leave the hospital, behave in an aggressive or truculent manner. A busy social worker then tends to accept what the patient says at its face value and turn to the job of finding accommodation for someone who will be more grateful.

'Prison is, paradoxically, the nearest to what these people really need. The standard of living there is low and there is an orderly structured existence which gives them security. Some are aware of this, and so we find still going through the law courts a tragic number of cases of things like bricks being thrown through a window, in sight of a constable, in order to get back inside. Such things are especially common as Christmas approaches.'

'Heark, heark the dogs do bark, the beggars are come to town.'
That was the old treatment for down and outs. The dogs barked because the beggars were going to be driven over the parish boundary. We don't do that so much now. Where we used to move them on, now we settle them down. The Spikes, that network of free Reception Centres, a day's walk apart, once covered nearly the whole of Britain and thus made possible a life of tramping. But so many have been closed that it's no longer possible to get from one to the other on your own feet. Now, in mental hospitals, prison, or in the vast halls of Common Lodging Houses, we do violence to our failures in a different way.

Can it be that our State Institutions often do precisely the reverse of what they set out to do? That those whom they were designed to help they punish?

'There was this fellow, he'd had sixty convictions in seventy years. The most recent time they got him, it was for travelling on the railways without paying his fare. He said he'd decided to leave London, to try to get somewhere cleaner. He was given the choice of a ten pound fine or two months in the nick. And he chose the nick.'

A dosser says, 'I used to go out to have a drink and I used to get with me friends and spend it all in the bar. I couldn't stop meself you see. I used to say, "What'll you have?" And if they said, "A pint," I'd say, "No, have a shortie." Treat all the bar. And in those days I was especially generous to tramps I was. I was a good boy to the tramps. You know, I'd always see that they was all right.

'One day my boss he asked me, "How much do you give your wife?" And I told him. So he said, "O.K. I'll keep that amount back from your wages."

'And I stuck it for three weeks but then I gave up because I didn't like it, giving it all to the wife. So I came to live here.'

An old dosser says, 'It is pretty depressing sometimes, I'd do work if I could find it. For instance the other day I heard tell of work that was going about ten mile from here. So I walked over. And there was five men wanted and only two turned up.

'So I thought, that's all right then.

'But when my name came up, age sixty-two, he said, "Oh no, that's no go, you see I want someone that can stick with the job, but you'll be leaving it in a year or so. So what use are you to us?" '

Another dosser says, 'It's a good life, oh yes. But I often think, if I'd of known what the future would hold, in store I mean, I'd never of taken on living. Oh, no life, no life for me.'

Ian Henderson tells me, 'Until recently it was believed that the necessary machinery existed for solving the down and out problem. It was thought that with the increase in our affluence and the improvement in our social services, the down and out would give up the ghost and fade away. But he refuses to do this. It may even be that he is a sort of waste product of affluence. His problem is social, not economic. He fears, and retreats from, the necessity to make decisions which is a feature of our technological and predominantly urban society.

'Decision making has become so complicated that he opts out of even basic decisions affecting food and shelter. Because social relationships have become impersonal (barter replaced by the village shop replaced by the supermarket), it is much easier to drop out.'

Jerome Liss, the psychiatrist, tells me, 'Human beings are like magnetised balls floating on an ocean surface. One ball will keep you up but you'll probably be putting overmuch pressure on it. A group of balls will support you well. But without any balls, you'll sink.' Human beings *need* this magnetised field.

But our society provides no agglomeration of these cohesive balls. We may in fact be geared to *producing* the down and out, not preventing him.

A study of vagrancy in the city of Birmingham claimed, 'There has been a great increase in the number of patients of no fixed abode admitted to mental hospitals in the Birmingham region in the last ten years.'*

The Unknown Citizen, by Tony Parker,§ describes the predicament of this type of person.

'I cannot think, I have not been equipped by life for the process of rational thought. I have never had the sun of being loved for who I was. For me there is no release. My mind is a confused no-man's-land of water-logged craters and barbed wire, collapsed dug-outs and uncharted wastes of mud; shrouded in a pall of dark, through which I flounder perpetually, frightened and alone. Had I died in a war, in conditions like these, I might have been buried as the Unknown Soldier. But I live in your society like this, and I am the Unknown Citizen.'

A psychiatrist has done research into the theory that humans come in two basic types. One can maintain a mental set without distraction, solves problems with a clearly observable set of responses, articulates information in a segmented, analytical, structured way. The other is hypersensitive, responds to peripheral cues, is more imaginative and yielding to all kinds of stimulation. The first might become a scientist or executive, the second an artist or mystic.

Our State is orientated towards the first and often punishes the second. People emerge from lunatic asylums, from prison, unable to cope, and return to these same places, still unable to cope.

In Victorian times there was, 'Forming a substratum below even the meanest of artisan classes . . . an outcast and forgotten people.'

And Dickens describes, 'A crowd of foul existence that crawls in and out of gaps in walls and boards and coils itself to sleep in maggot numbers . . . sowing more evil in its every footprint than all the fine gentlemen in office shall set right in five hundred years.'

These people are still with us. Up to ten thousand habitually or occasionally sleep rough.*

Spikes (Reception Centres) and kiphouses (or dosshouses) between them have about thirty-five thousand beds in the whole of Britain.† To the dossers occupying these must be added those thousands who are in mental hospital or prison.§

Anton Wallich-Clifford of the Simon Community puts the figure of those for whom there exist no social services of which they could take advantage, at about one hundred thousand.

The National Association of Voluntary Hostels** now arrange nearly 1,000 'placements' for such people every year.* About one-third of these placements are people who come from hospitals or psychiatric hospitals. There are alcoholics, drug addicts, mentally disturbed, sub-normal, epileptics, physically handicapped, probationers, on remand, from detention centre, from Approved School, Borstal, ex-prisoners, pregnant and/or unmarried mothers, estranged and/or expectant wives, children in care, homeless families.

Christian Action have established hostels for such people, and describe them in a handout, as follows, 'Many live a shiftless existence, moving restlessly from one lodging house to another.

'Others are to be found in psychiatric and general hospitals, casualty departments, police stations and in prison. Yet others have no other alternative but to sleep rough in doorways or all-night launderettes, telephone kiosks, and on the bare wooden benches of the main line railway stations.'*

The Cyrenians are another organisation who, of recent months, have built up an impressive network of hostels.*

The Spike stood up against the grey sky, stuck between the railway lines, three tall wings with the central one like a church, enclosed by barbed wire and tall walls, joined by colonnades, long arches with spindly ironwork.*

I'd come down here on foot, past the tenements and the terraced houses, reaching what must have been green fields when the Spike was built, and which now were line after line of smug suburban dwellings, their gardens filled with sweetly smelling shrubs, and the streets outside littered with abandoned motors.

I called in at the front lodge of the huge monastery-like building and the man there told me to go round the back. I walked round the block and came to a tall wooden fence with barbed wire round the top, and a gap in the fence.

I was in a tarmac quad, triangular, brightly lit with spot-lights giving it an unreal silver look. At one end was a booth, brightly lit, with figures silhouetted against the windows.

Someone directed me to a waiting room, completely dark, filled with men lying on the concrete floor, sprawled on chairs. From one figure, sprawled along three chairs, there came a resonant snoring. There was a large bell fixed to the wall above the door. Now it pealed loudly. Two figures uncurled themselves from a couple of chairs and slouched out of the doorway.

The snoring continued.

The bell pealed again, loudly, and a man lying in a corner began to swear raggedly. Two more men got up and slouched out of the door.

The bell pealed again.

About an hour later it was my turn. I walked across the yard and into the booth. At the level of my chin there was a window covered with silver mesh. A neon tube shone into my face.

After being sent back because I'd not brought my National Insurance card, the bell rang again and I was called back to the grille. Inside the window was a fat, bald man in his shirtsleeves, with sad blue steady eyes.

'Cards please.' He held out his hand at the end of its hairy wrist.

'Sorry, I haven't got them.'

The man shouted, 'Why? Where are they?'

'Haven't got them. I lost them.'

'Go and find them.'

'I told you, I can't.'

'Go and find them! Go! Go and find them!'

'Listen. . . . '

'Go back! I don't want you here! Go back! Go back to the waiting room.'

I went back.

There were only four of us left in the waiting room now. The bell rang again, but because he had told us to wait, we didn't move. The bell rang again, deafeningly. Finally, there was a shout, 'Do you want beds or don't you?'

Back in front of the grille. Details, age, occupation, next of kin. Why here? Because homeless. Bed ticket Number II, into a hot room smelling of disinfectant. A Greek in a rough khaki overall said, 'Take off your shirt and vest and show them me.'

He peered at them under a lamp.

'Now your socks.'

He tossed me a towel, 'Leave them here. I'll have to disinfect them. Now go and have a shower.'

A man in the next shower to me said, 'That's a relief. That's the first wash I had for three weeks.'

When I was through with the tepid shower he gave me some rough ill-fitting old clothes and I went on to the next room where there was a counter on which sat a tureen of watery soup and some pieces of bread.

After eating the bread and the soup, I picked up three blankets, then went up a long flight of stairs to a door which had my number on it. Opened it. A vast room filled with eighty sleeping figures, and a faint orange glow. Stench. An occasional voice crying out as if in pain.

I laid out the three blankets on the waterproof mattress. My shoes went under the pillow. I fell asleep.

Next morning, I joined the crowd of men in the cubicles filled with washbasins. A notice said, 'All men must wash and shave before breakfast. By Order.' The dawn was coming and down the iron staircase stumbled a long line of shambling men, stumbling down out of the sky with their blankets, some dropping them down from the fire escapes onto the asphalt below.

The yard was filling up with even more men. Then a bell rang and hundreds of men piled into the vast hall, sat at long scrubbed tables, elbow to elbow, and breakfast was passed along.

A pleasant room in which a fire was brightly burning. I sat with a doctor* at a green baize-covered table. The first down and out entered.

'Are you in work now?'

'Oh, yes, sir.'

'What are you doing?'

'I'm doing the buckets and that outside the bathroom. And swilling down the tiles.'

'Oh, so you work in here?'

'Yes.'

'Did you ever try for work outside?'

'Yes, sir.'

'Were they kind to you?'

'No, sir.'

'Did they offer you any work?'

'No. Said I was too old.'

'Did they go by how old you are or how old you look?'

'Don't know, sir.'

'All right, we'll let you stay here through the winter and then turn you out when the summer comes. That all right?'

A smile of joy lit up the old man's face.

'The next one's deaf. He shouts like anything, but he can't hear a thing,' said the assistant.

'Oh yes. I remember. He worked in an ammunition factory, didn't he, and it blew up, and he didn't get a pension. You're almost the oldest inhabitant?'

The old man shouted, 'Sorry, I can hear what you're saying, sir. I can hear what you're saying. I can hear what you're saying sir.'

But it was quite clear that he couldn't.

'I said, You're almost the oldest inhabitant here!'

'Oh, yes, sir. Yes sir, yes sir,' cried the old man, still not hearing.

'Here comes another deaf one.'

'He's deaf and dumb?'

'Yes.'

'Born deaf and dumb.'

'No, he's not, he was born deaf, hence dumb. He could speak if he were taught. But it's a bit late now, I suppose.'

39

He shouted, 'What is your work?'

But the old man, locked in his own particular silence, made no sign of having heard. The doctor clutched him roughly by the shoulder and made violent spade-shovelling gestures and then blinked at him questioningly. The man shook his head violently, and then made vigorous boot-repairing gestures.

Another man, 'Cough, cough, cough, cough, then come the phlegm.' This man had black hair, black eyes protruding from pink lids. A terrible cough.

'Have you tried for work?'

'No, I've shrunk. I've been working. I like work but these days I don't feel too good. Dunno why. I've shrunk. I feel better when I'm drunk.'

'Would you like me to try to find you a place here?'

'Oh, yes,' said the old man, his face lighting up. He went out. 'That,' said the doctor, 'was lightweight champion for England.'

The last man was younger than the others. 'Well, what are you doing here?' asked the doctor.

The young man said, with tears in his eyes. 'Thrown me out of home they have, me Dad turned me out. He's got a woman living there. He turned me out.'

'Were you in work?'

'Well, yes, I was in work, but being a bit slow I lost me job, and me Dad said he couldn't stand me sitting around all day.'

'How old are you?'

'Well, I'm twenty-eight years of age. I shouldn't be here, I should be somewhere else. I should. I should be somewhere else.'

'You get a lot of that,' said the doctor when he'd gone out. 'They stay with their parents till the parents die and after that they can't fend for themselves.'

'Oh yes, this is the best place. The best place I've been in. Long as I can stay here I'll be very, very happy. Only one thing else I'd like. A room of me own.'

Her face is lined and seamed with many ages of dirt. The rest of her is hidden beneath layer after layer of shapeless clothes, from the bottom of which protrude large boots.

She is in the Christian Action Hostel for Homeless Women in Lambeth High Street. It is not too tidy nor too big. Its inhabitants sleep in dormitories, or on the floor if they wish.

A girl with a dark quiet intensity about her told me, 'My Dad said to me, he said, "From now on you do what I tell you to. You won't do what you want to do. You do what I say."

'You see my Mum had died on me up in Manchester, and there was no one to look after me, so my Dad came up to get me, and that's what he said as we went down in the train, and then he belted me round the ear.

'And when we got back he used to go with me – you know.'

Another girl told me, 'I was one of ten taken into care and protection because they said I was under the influence of my elder brothers. My father was alcoholic and my Mum was mentally ill.

'I had seven months nursing training, then they said I was unfit due to a heart murmur. I met a fella and I thought I loved him, and he me. I thought it was sex and excitement I was after but now, looking back, I see it was only affection. I met another man. His name was Jimmy and we got married. But I couldn't get pregnant again although I'd had a child by the first man. Then at last I did become pregnant and not so long after that I started bleeding.

'I went to see the doctor and he said, "You'd better go to bed and stay there." But the next day when I was in bed I heard my first kid screaming, in the next room. I jumped out of bed and saw my husband attacking the baby with a fork. And then as I was restraining him the bleeding started again and I had a miscarriage.

'I took the kid with me because I didn't think it was safe to leave him there. But my husband went to the school one afternoon and took him away. So, then I went down to Eastbourne and lived with my Mum. I took too many aspirin and the police took me to the Station. I came back and I got into a hostel in London but I was unhappy there and I fell back with my rent. I went to the social security but they couldn't help me and I don't know why I did it, but just there where I was I slashed my wrist. They let me into a mental institution. But now I've had a bit of luck. I've got into the Christian Hostel.'

'The thing is, we really ought to throw her out.'

'Yes, but the trouble is no one else will take her.'

Some of the staff were discussing one of the girls.

'At this place they're only meant to stay two weeks.'

'Yes. But if we throw her out of here, it really is the gutter. I know she's embarrassing to have around. She does this exhibitionist thing, Go, on, kill me, kill me.'

'We did get her a job in the city at one point, washing dishes, but she lost her epileptic tablets, and had a fit, so she came back. She annoys you, that's the trouble, she won't leave you alone. She hangs on to you. She drains you. She just won't leave you

41

alone. Then she gets into towering rages, stamps her feet, throws herself around. Then she stands in the street, makes verbal passes at men, won't let them go by, exposes herself, it's embarrassing.'

A man said, 'Yes, she even said to me, "Are you taking me out?", something like that.'

'Is she attractive to men, though? I can't really believe it. She seems to get men none the less.'

'But how, and where does she take them to?'

'Oh, just on the back seat of their car. I've seen her chatting up men in the street.'

'But she can't be attractive, she has no teeth in the front of her mouth.'

'She's young. That's enough.'

A violent bumping noise was heard. 'Good heavens, what's that?'

'It's all right, that's just Lil cleaning up.'

'What sort of cleaning, for goodness sake? She sounds as if she's breaking the place down.'

'Oh, Lil never has been particularly quiet in her activities.'

'Anyway, to get back to Trudi, she wants to be kept till the tenth. Can we really keep her till then? She's such a disrupting element to the other people in the hostel. The moment I tell her to leave she indulges in fits of screaming. The other day she came in and said to me, "I'm going to keep an exact record of all my fits. And then I'm going to write to the newspapers about them." I said, "But they won't be interested in your fits." And she said, "If they're not, then they ought to be."'

'At any rate it's better now than it was in the summer. Then she used to wear hip-length dresses and stockings, walking along laughing and talking. She's very sweet in a way, but of course she is very disturbed.'

The girl who told me of her father having sexual intercourse with her said, 'When my father was going with me I used to cry sometimes, Oh I want me Mum, I want me Mum. I know they say that somebody who is hurt themselves will try to hurt others. I know it but still I try to hurt them.

'Sometimes I wish so much to be back in the psychiatric. I wanted to be back so much I broke a window so they'd have to put me there. But the psychiatrist said I was all right, he didn't want his bed blocked, I must go. They gave me ECT. They put these things on my ear, you know, one electrode on one ear and the other on the other, and then they switched it on and still I get convulsions when I remember it. No, I know that I was under

42

sedation, but I knew what they were doing all the same. When I first came to the hostel it was as if there was no stuffing in me, I used to just sit around, and crack my bones, it's a funny habit, I can wrench one bone against another. I used to do it till they went mad. But I don't do it so much now – quite. I wanted to get back so bad.

'I don't know what's got into me. I nicked my friend's social security vouchers, I swallowed tablets, I was sick, and then I scooped the sick up back off the floor. I drank disinfectant, I know it was to try to get me back into hospital. I was confused. I was in Barnardo's long ago, I'd like to go back there now. But those places are for children, aren't they?'

'Leave me alone! Leave my mind alone!'

The most bizarre of all the dormitories is number five. One of the inhabitants is an alcoholic old lady who staggers down in the middle of the night, completely sloshed, to complain of the exhibitionist girl running naked round the house. Another is the lady who walks about all night.

'You can't walk around all the time, it wakes the others up.'

'Yes, but I have to, you see, my doctor says it's most important for me to be able to walk about, most important.'

And the epileptic girl wanders about exposing herself to anybody who'll look or who won't look.

As we sat in the office in the middle of the night, an old lady came down, 'I have to leave. I have to leave! I'm sorry, it's an unfortunate romance, I can't talk about it but I've got to go right now.'

Outside it was a snowy winter's night. 'Are you sure you want to go now?' asked one of the attendants.

'Yes, I've got to go, I've got to! I'm sorry, I've fallen so deeply now that I can't get out any other way. Otherwise I'll go off my head.'

And now an old lady staggered in drunk, apologising about the night before and saying that she can't stand Trudi exposing herself, that it drives her to drink.

Another girl came in. She said, 'I've just been up the dilly. Everybody's there, it's crazy, they're just all stoned, just lying around. I don't know what's happening to this country. I think everybody's going to be overwhelmed, we're all going to be stoned, the Chinese will get us!'

Trudi called in at the office, 'Please, I've got a sore on my bottom, will you dress it?'

'All right, Trudi, I'll do a deal with you. I'll dress your bottom if you'll agree to wash your face every day.'

'What do you remember of your youth in a children's home?' I asked a girl.

'Well, I remember stealing a toy from a boy.'

'Why did you steal it?'

'Because I hated him.'

'Why did you hate him?'

'I hated him because he was happy.'

'Why?'

'Because he came from a happy home, and I came from an unhappy home. I don't know why. I only know I hated him. When I went out to play with him, his Mum said he mustn't play with me or mix with me. And that made me frantic.'

Major Scott, the pleasant white-haired lady who runs the Salvation Army Hostel for destitute and homeless women at Hopetown in London's East End, invited me to be there during the weekly rent collection.

A dormitory bed in this place costs thirty pence a night. A cubicle costs thirty-five pence, and a private room, forty pence a night.

The first woman who came in to pay her rent was a coloured lady, who had got a letter from her son of seventeen who was asking her for money with which to get to Kingston, Jamaica.

'Don't give him too much,' said the Major.

After the woman had gone out she said, 'They say that that lady came here a long while ago, with her child, in a bad way. Her husband had been beating her up. After a night here she said she felt stronger so she went back home but found him in bed with a white girl.

'He exploited her through the whole of that marriage, and now it seems the son is doing the same. He's constantly writing, asking her for money.'

The next woman had a severe, sad, gaunt face, and wore a cap like a candle extinguisher. Gravely she placed the money on Major Scott's desk.

The Major said, aside to me, 'That lady never speaks. And we don't know who she is. Apparently she was a model. But now she never speaks.'

She asked the next lady, 'How long have you been here?'

'I don't know.'

'Well, would it be twenty years? Were you here in Major Sey-

44

mour's time?'

'Oh yes, I remember the Major.'

'Then you must have been here for twenty years.'

On the table there was a large bottle for money.

'Sometimes they put something aside from their money to pay for the colour television.'

There were various letters waiting for the next woman, all from Her Majesty.

'Oh dear, it must be for their income tax,' said the old lady, 'they're always writing to me about that. So last time I wrote to them and said, "Can't pay no income tax. I've got no money for you to take, maybe you can take my life." '

'Now, you mustn't talk like that,' said the Major.

When she'd gone out the Major said, 'As you heard she has a speech defect, and this gets worse when she's nervous. She finds it hard to express herself, so when she goes for a job she can't really make contact. She could do the job very well but she can't explain this to her employers, so she doesn't get the job. She's got a son at one of our men's hostels. We don't allow men and women to mix, so they go out and sit in the park, sometimes, together.

'We have to have a rule here that after three months the young girls with children must go (although of course we'd never turn them out with nowhere else to go).

'If I had to mention one special quality which I feel the girls here possess, it's that they are not strong enough to fight.

'The pressure on places is immense. I could easily fill another hostel the same size as this. And I'd like that. If I had another hostel I'd sort out the workers from the rest. I'd have one hostel just for the workers.

'We have a wing here that we call the "Cathy Wing". Sometimes we have to turn away four or five Cathies a day.

'One problem about the unmarried mothers here is that they can get their children into a nursery but a nursery doesn't take a child for the whole day. So Mum can't get a full-time job, she can only get a part-time job, and at that rate she realizes that she'd be better off on social security.

'This is a society that does things by proxy. People ring us up and say things like, "There's an old woman seems to be dying in a doorway, can't you do something, can't you do something for her?" It never occurs to them to do something for her themselves.

'I say to them, Well can't *you* do something for her? And, secondly, is she *willing* for something to be done for her?

'One old woman was literally carried in by the police one night.

It had never occurred to them to help the poor old thing themselves.'

Another lady in Salvation Army uniform came in, older than Major Scott. Major Scott introduced her and said, 'This lady, Auntie, is a Brigadier and she does our *War Cry* sales. In the old days when the girls had to pay for their keep by sewing, she used to take the sewing out round the neighbourhood to sell it. She's very good. Last Christmas she went round the shops and she brought back fifty-five pounds.

'The women here are very sweet to each other. Some of the old ones are orientated towards hatred, but mainly they are very sweet to each other, unlike the men's hostels where I'm told the atmosphere is more hostile.

'One of the women here is a naughty old thing, she's a thief, she takes our soap and sells it. We don't allow smoking, but she likes a cigarette, so the whole of the back of her coat has been burnt where she hides it when I come in.

'The ladies pay five pence a week for their lockers. Sometimes we have to clean them out because they keep all kinds of food which goes rotten.

'Even so, in spite of this clean up, we do have mice here. The cats wait in the corridors by night, watching to catch them.'

An old stooping woman came in to pay her rent. Major Scott said, 'She used to chain smoke, and when she first came she was completely filthy. Her sister had kept her in a room in a starved condition and used to cash in her old-age pension and spend it all herself. One day her boys decided to go and see how she was, and they were so horrified that they brought her here. We didn't let any of the other ladies see her before we'd given her a bath and smartened her up. And now she stands far straighter and she's become happy. But she never ventures out.

'We have someone here also that no one knows who she is. What we do know is that she walked out on her husband and two children, but she won't say anything more than that. She's the nicest old thing, she works in the kitchen. Sometimes I say to her, "Have you done something you're ashamed of? Please tell me who you are. I wouldn't tell or hold it against you." But she just says, "One day I'll tell you, but not now. You know that if I'm an embarrassment to you, I'll go."

' "No we don't want you to go. But I wish you'd tell me."

' "Not now. One day I'll tell you, but not now."

'On Wednesday evenings we have entertainments. Some Wednesdays we have the Salvation Army Evangelical Choir from

Redhill. On another night we might have a musical Salvation Army family. Then on another occasion we may have the editor of *The Deliverer* speaking to us. We have expeditions as well. For instance, one year we went to the Ice Show at Wembley.

'When I first took over control here I couldn't understand why everyone looked so fearful when they saw me. Then someone told me. The rumour had gone round that I planned to send the older ones away to an old people's home. But I told them that they needn't fear, I wouldn't.

'I wouldn't do that to them because once you take an old person's pension book from her that's the last bit of their independence gone. They're happier here than in an old people's home.

'There is one old lady who every night says her prayers, kneeling by the bed, and her ritual is that then she empties her purse out on the bed and counts the money over, and then she says more prayers.'

A Captain came in and told her there was someone waiting outside to see her. Major Scott went out and then I heard her voice, 'Listen! Don't you dare do that again, promise to come and see your girl-friend and then don't come. She was waiting several hours out here for you to come last night with the children. And then you never came! How can you do that to her?'

Somebody rang up from an office party offering some sandwiches.

'Well, we could use them if you'll give them to us, and if you'll get them to us.'

She continued to talk to me, 'There was a lady who'd been in prison for much of her life, and she came here with the idea that she would just stay one night and then go on to an ex-prisoner's hostel. But after a day, she said, "Please can I stay here, I've made so many friends here, and they're not ex-prisoners either, they don't know I've been inside and it's so nice for me!" '

There are pigeons flying amongst the spindly tables of this vast dining-hall-cum-living room. Here, in Bruce House, a local authority lodging house, is one of the old-fashioned hotplates and men are crowding all round it. A bearded man is stirring up a disgusting looking mess in a frying-pan, and in a large tin a noxious stew made from vegetables is cooking. Another man, one of whose feet has been securely wrapped in a polythene bag tied with string round his ankle, is trying to grill bacon in the top of a tin that formerly held Snowcem. The pigeons go where they want through the smoky atmosphere, picking up titbits.

'Fuck you!' shouts the bearded man by the hotplate.

'Double fuck you!' shouts another man back.

And they continue to shout raggedly at each other. Then one man commits an act of assault upon his friend. 'Double fuck you, I'll get your fucking stick from out your fucking flies,' he shouts.

There is a violent struggle at the end of which the man's flies are ripped open.

I notice as if by way of comment in another hostel a notice which says, 'Naked lights are forbidden in the bedrooms'.

At one time all lodging houses had hotplates, but now most of them have gone. And the sheets seemed clean on the morning I called. This place costs thirty-five pence a night. There are other notices, 'Prevention of consumption – do not spit'. A notice in the entrance hall says, 'House Full'. And another notice threatens eviction to those who fail to inform the management of their need for medicinal baths and those who are found to be verminous. Beyond this was a green rack criss-crossed with black lace and filled with letters, all from Her Majesty.

In a farther room there was a vast Victorianate stove and a group of men sitting, most of them asleep, some drunk, some blotto on the fatal wine of indolence, round it. One man would not keep quiet. 'Aw fuck,' he kept on shouting. The ceiling was hung with battered neon lights in light yellow or light orange, their two shades a little broken round the corners. 'Let other folk go to sleep!' cried someone else. And in another group the conversation had turned to the subject of justice.

A young man with very long hair said, 'They envy me my hair. That's what it's all about. Sexual jealousy.' He smiled confidently as he lounged back in his chair. 'The law stopped me at Piccadilly, they claimed they'd found cannabis on me, but I said, Well, I was given it by a man I didn't know. I've been drifting round England, they said, You haven't got a source of income? No.'

All the time that he talked he smiled.

'We lived in the poorer part of Belfast, then I came to London to look for work. But I didn't get it, they envied me my hair, that was the trouble. I feel lost, I told 'em, that's it. I've asked for work. And I just went on smiling, you know, well, here I am and isn't it great, and the Magistrate he give me a long talk about nothing, how it was up to me to pull myself out of the rut, he was going to fine me twelve quid, to pay this I'd have to get myself a job. I think the law's off its head, really, no sane society could have laws like this.

'Cannabis is far less harmful than alcohol, and as for wandering around, why shouldn't I?'

Many of the thousands of men in Britain's dosshouses are in need of help.

These are the people whose need is so great that they cannot express it in the proper form – they cannot 'dress-up', in mind or body, to express their need in the requisite mode.

There are many things that we could attempt to do for these men and some ways that we could try to use them. At the moment we are doing little but try to enclose them in a world of Spikes and lodging houses which we then sometimes even close down in the rather eccentric hope that their inmates will vanish with them.

Sir,
    We citizens of the abyss know that society is ranged against us. We are 'nobodies' with no help from nowhere.
        Asses, swine, have litter spread,
        And with fitting food are fed.
        All things but one –
        Thou O Englishman, has none.
No bed for the night, if you haven't got four bob.

As automation gets under way it is likely that there'll be more and more of these dropouts, men and women without work, coming to the towns, equipped only with their hands and an infinite leisure.

Sir,
    This is a very colourful account of some 'dossers' *but not all*. Very many of these men are hard working, and tramp from town to town, not all are 'Jake Wallako' or lie abouts, many do not qualify for social security owing to various reasons. Many have fought in two World Wars, and keep themselves as clean as they can, clothes may be shabby, they are generally bought from some rubbish tip, many live on less than thirty shillings a week, or shall we say exist.

After the First World War there were hundreds of thousands on Tramp. All 'Spikes' or casual wards were open, some only a few miles between each other, all were full every night, and hundreds sleeping rough doing a Skipper as well. At these places you did a few hours work for your bed and food, wood chopping or similar, and went on your way the next morning. After the Second World War, there were still vast numbers of unwanted men on the road. Conditions however were not quite so bad. The Government then closed many hundreds of 'Spikes' all over the country. Today there are only a few dozen open, and these are often sixty or seventy miles apart. The so-called private 'Kips', ever dear to the professional Tramp, are few and far between it is a good thing we have a few left because Hostels are sometimes full and there is nowhere else to go. There are Tramp colonies outside most large Towns, many however, never go near these places or Hostels, they sleep 'rough' all the year round and they are willing to work if they can get it. Regarding the Men on the road, you meet all types, there is the collar and tie man and the man with the muffler. Some have good Education.

A Dosser.

'Wine Drinkers Keep Out', read the scrawled notice on the decrepit wall. Beneath it on the scarred stone steps lay sprawled an elderly man. His filthy overcoat and tattered trousers fell aside to reveal an artificial leg. A bottle of surgical meths lay shattered on the ground beside him.

Inside the dosshouse, three or four dossers were waiting for food and a mean, spectacled, queer looking man, wearing a white overall, with a white and pink blotched fish-like face, was speaking to those in front of him with sarcastic politeness. 'Sorry, I've only got soup. Yes that's all. You can't have anything else. Right. Well, do you want to spend your breakfast tickets on soup?'

'Yes, one soup, please.'

'No. We don't do that.'

'Just one soup.'

'No, we don't give change, you'll have to have the lot. It's soup and two slices for a tanner, so that's three soups.'

The St Mungo Community is in a terraced house in Home Road, Battersea, and other London houses.

The passage, as you go in through the door, is stacked high with reject food of various sorts, piles and piles of grapes, loaves, in shiny packages, crushed into various uncouth shapes.

I climb upstairs, peering into the dormitory where two-tier bunk beds stand, covered with a squalor of bedclothes.

On the top floor the roof slants down low over an attractive room containing a fish tank where various types of fish endlessly revolve, and comfortable mattresses are laid on the floor.

A doctor whom I met here tells me, 'The derelict "inadequate" can be a man more intelligent than the rest, a man to whom violence has been done. He is more intelligent so he is able to perceive the contradictions in his upbringing.

'His mother behaves cruelly to him; but in church he is taught that you must not say or do an unkind thing. An unintelligent child won't notice this, but in the case of an intelligent child, the confusion kills him spiritually.

'I know a young girl who has had seventy boy-friends. She's trying to hurt her parents. If she, or I for her, can hurt them enough, then she will get better.

'But some forms of schizophrenia are the product of drugs. We have an old lady who comes to us twice a week and we give her a stimulant and she has a sort of sexual experience and as a result of this she goes away happy and untense.

'Somebody I knew quite well suffered depression and we gave her a drug. She seemed much better in herself. But, after a while, as we were watching black and white T.V. she suddenly said, "I don't like all those colours." And then she saw a policeman on the screen, "Help, they're coming for me!"

'So we realised that although the drug had calmed her down a bit it had also turned her into a schizophrenic. But did it matter? That lady had been given some sort of zest for life.'

Jim Horne, the man who runs the St Mungo Community, told me, 'We have been lent a railway arch, filled with rubbish, in the East End of London. It is knee deep in slime. You have to stand in your gum boots, which we've been given free, but this will enable us to meet we hope some of the more intelligent ones who've dropped out. Then they can come back to the hostel and be helped to see things straight, and we'll send them back to the bomb site and embankments to help others.

'What we do at the hostel is help the inadequate people until they reach a point at which they can begin to confront their own problems. But we can't help them beyond that. They reach the point at which they know that they're ready to take a step up. But they're not able to. Instead, the knowledge that they should take a step up but that there's nowhere for them to go may send them back to square one, to drinking or pushing.

'So often,' said the doctor, 'they are what they are because of something that happened in an institution. Soon there's going to be an explosion of public concern about conditions in institutions in general. You can hardly pick up a paper without seeing a reference to brutality in some institution.

'I didn't believe the first person who came out of a Mental Hospital and described the sort of things that went on there. But when you get three or more people coming out with these same stories, then you do begin to believe them.

'The worst thing that a parent can ever do to his child, perhaps, is to tell him that they wish he hadn't been born. And yet you hear it all the time, even in court, mothers are saying this about their children.'

Jim Horne is a man most worthy of admiration. He responded in a very personal way to what he saw going on around him. Now he runs no less than six London hostels, and organises the exacting nightly soup run that I have already described.

Anton Wallich-Clifford has been running hostels like this for some years now and was the originator of many new ideas in Britain. He told me, 'The idea behind most places like this is that the man will be given a refresher course, enabling him to turn into a decent citizen again. There is always the idea that, ultimately, he will return to the world. Finally turning him out only continues the series of rejections that such a person has had through life. Our aim is different. We want to create a series of hostels so arranged that no one will ever need to leave them.

'I believe that it is precisely the hopeless cases, of whom people say, when they first come to us, "You'll be lumbered with them for life," who will be saying, a few years later, "That looks an interesting job I see advertised, I think I'll go for it."

'The fact that we have not pressurised them will enable them to return to society in their own good time.'

The hostel which the Simon Community runs at Malden Road, and various other houses, are fairly tatty buildings containing 'social inadequates' and also 'helpers', and homeless families.

'We feel that the we/they attitude to helping somebody is wrong. The barrier set up by the usual form of social worker, i.e. a desk, is completely wrong and so, we feel, is the normal form of help which is like dropping a rope down a well and saying, "Hang on to this and we'll pull you up." Our attitude is that we should get down into the well and help push from alongside these people.

'The residents are referred to us from various voluntary and statutory bodies, the Samaritans, probation officers, hospitals, social workers, and priests. They come from all walks of life. They all share the problems of some sort of social inadequacy.

'The neighbours help us to provide food. Recently an Indian family rang us up late at night and said that they had had a burial feast. There was a great deal of food left over, would we like to go and collect this. So we sent one of our workers round.

'The local shopkeepers also help. The butcher keeps us supplied with meat at very much reduced prices, usually something he isn't selling particularly well that day.

'Anton Wallich-Clifford decided to leave the desk-bound elite, and gave up his professional career to be very much more on the coal-face, working with the inadequate at their level.

'The Simon Community is perhaps best known for its work with the crude spirit drinker, in other words, the sort of person drinking methylated spirits, melted down boot polish, eau de cologne, diesel oil, etc. and also for its work with the drug addict, and it is because of its more sensational news value that this part of our work has tended to be most reported.

'In actual fact, we work with the whole field of social inadequacy, having set up homes in the past for such widely varying cases as unmarried mothers, schizophrenics, psychopaths, homosexuals, recidivist prisoners and of course the ever increasing number of recidivist mental patients.'

Anton is well known for his eccentricity. 'When he's taken by backers for his projects into restaurants he goes in in his foulest clothes, he doesn't mind what he wears, he gets out his old pipe and his penknife, he scrapes away at the pipe completely unconcerned. His mother used to give him a shilling every now and again when he was a boy and he would go off into the village until he saw some old tramp and then he'd give it to him.'

Anton was the originator of so many of the ideas which are now coming to be accepted in the world of those who care for Britain's down and outs.

Years before anyone else had thought of these things, he was advocating those ideas which now form the currency of enlightened people.

Again and again I find, on investigating some setup, that the man who runs it was trained by Anton Wallich-Clifford.

He is one of those rare people who, again and again, comes up with ideas which sound cranky when they are first enunciated, but ten years later can be found to have passed into the currency of the thinking of liberated people.

One of his disciples, and a man who now runs a large network of small permissive hostels, is Tom Gifford of the Cyrenians.

This small and energetic Scotsman has recently been moving up and down Britain like a ball of fire, together with wife and dog, sprinkling out insults and compliments to Local Authorities, students, and all others who may have relevance to this world of the down and out.

With Tom, I have been touring, lecturing and showing the film of 'Edna the Inebriate Woman' for fund-raising, recruitment, and information purposes.

Tom is in the work, he says, 'because he cares about humans.'

He has carried the caring into a practical field. His hostels, stretching up and down the land, are havens amidst a desert of non-caring.

I have been in many of his houses and find the experience always intensely moving. I hope that the empire of hostels that he now services will go from strength to strength.

'The Manor House. Single Bedded Rooms if Desired. Good Food at Lowest Prices'.

It was a well-proportioned late Georgian building, set back from the road, the notice painted across its front in nice black letters.

I lingered a moment on the pavement, sizing it up. It was late now, I'd been searching since two, and so far I'd not found a bed in a dosshouse. The front door was shut. In a low window to the left of it I could see innumerable men squashed together, some munching. From a space under steps leading to the door two figures staggered out and erupted into the street beside me. As I was still standing irresolute a Pole staggered up to me, big finger splayed against his pouting pink lips, 'O.K. Paddy, say nothing, come on, quick, say nothing.' He clutched my arm. I recoiled a little from the drunken old man. He detected my hesitation and croaked severely, '*Say nothing*. Come on in. *Say nothing*. I help you! Help someone in trouble! Nothing else! You think I'm a queer don't you? Well I'm not. Nothing else!'

He dragged me across the forecourt and to a lower door, beneath the level of the front door, and kicked it open. The way was barred by a dark youth to whom he now spoke volubly in Yiddish. The boy stood back and we entered a filthy, panelled passage. The door to the left of us reverberated as if heavy boulders were being thrown against it. Two old dossers sprawled out.

'Canteen. You all right Paddy. You have a cup of tea Paddy, you come with me.' He strode towards the closed door, rattled on it with his knuckles, then kicked it. The door opened a fraction and a bearded face looked out.

'Paddies only.'

The door slammed shut.

'This *is* a Paddy!' He kicked the door again.

'Well actually,' I said, 'I'm not a Paddy.' For reply the Pole kicked the door with violence, again it opened fractionally, and a different face peered out. 'Canteen closed.'

Behind him I could see, amid the mêlée of jostling men, a dosser receiving a vast bacon sandwich.

'Sorry mate, canteen's closed.'

'I want to see the manager.'

'I *am* the manager.'

The door again shut and I said to the crestfallen man, 'It's all right, I didn't really want a cup of tea anyway.'

'Other place,' said the Pole. 'Paddies run that place.'

We started along the passage. Then the Pole clutched me by the shoulders. 'Listen, no more beds. I *have* bed.' He showed me the ticket. 'Got an idea! I sleep under bed! You sleep on top of the bed! All dark! No one see! Yes, is better! Not so cold!'

As I still held back he added, 'Nothing else wanted! I promise! Nothing else!'

At the end of the passage was a huge room with nine or ten long scrubbed tables in it, a T.V. feebly cackling, and the greatest collection of tramps I had ever seen, real old-fashioned tramps with long grey and yellow hair and huge boots, tramps singing, tramps gambling with cards or dice. There were two great, roaring, black fireplaces at which tramps were cooking up vegetables they'd picked up from the streets, tramps fighting with each other, tramps falling over with a heavy *thump*, tramps with gap teeth, tramps disdainfully watching the smooth-voiced chromium-imaged telly, tramps scouring out black pots and pans for the last taste of sustenance.

There must have been a hundred or so men in the room. A strange man, wearing a minute, smart, light blue sweater, too large grey trousers, smart brown shoes and a shirt, caught my attention. He held a kettle of water and was sprinkling it lightly over the floor.

The Pole led me to a farther room with another roaring fire and huge iron bars stretching into the room before it. He produced a thumbed pile of photographs and leafed over them with his fingers.

I looked, at first cursorily, and then with surprise. The man said, 'Oh yes, I was, yes, steamboat skipper.'

Photographs of various parts of the world, various ports, various girls, 'Yes, that was me wife. Yes. Took them I did.

There's me in me own car. Took them with me own camera.'

Now throughout this vast room the lights began to go out, and the tramps began to surge towards the door of the hall. Two men stood by the wicket, counting them as they went up the stairs. The Pole read from his ticket 'Front North'. 'Where's that? Where's Front North?' After various false starts we reached a room on the top floor, very cold, lit by moonlight with about thirty beds in it. The Pole said, 'Paddy, you get under there'. I climbed beneath the bed, lay on the cold ill-smelling floor. Men began to climb into their beds and there came the sound of snoring. Then the door opened and a torch flickered round the room, 'Come on, out of it! Out. *Out*!' A heavy foot prodded me. Sheepishly I got up and staggered out. I wanted to thank the kind Pole as I went out, but he was already snoring. Lying stiff and waxen, fully clothed, stretched out on his tin bed.

PART TWO

*Tales from the Nick and the Bin
and the Police Courts . . . and how they
so often do the reverse of what was intended*

I was beginning to form a picture of these 'citizens of the abyss', these social losers of our time.

Concern about the homeless family has been mobilized by 'Shelter' and the Squatters, and my own *Cathy* may have helped here, but this equally grave problem has so far received little attention – the problem of homeless single persons. Such people are often dubbed by society 'socially inadequate', and information about them is fairly hard to come by.

Kenneth Stoneley, representing the National Association of Voluntary Hostels, told me, 'Some thousands sleep out. Others will come from a meagre bed in a common lodging house or a psychiatric hospital, or prison, or some other type of institution.

'These are the exits from the down-and-out world. The fruitless havens for those who've fallen foul of "Britain basking in its contemporary affluence".'

The welfare state at the moment seems incapable of giving them much help which will be of any lasting use to them.

The latest detailed research on a national scale was carried out by the National Assistance Board in 1965 and 1966. Their figures are still probably, very broadly, accurate. The researchers for their report *Homeless Single Persons* (HMSO 1966) were interested in the number of people who sleep rough. Of the occupants of lodging houses and hostels, 1,120 slept rough frequently and 6,070 slept rough occasionally – or 28 per cent of the total. Of those in Spikes, 370 slept rough frequently and 926 occasionally – or 70 per cent. It is probable that fewer would admit to sleeping rough than actually did so, and since concealment is an important element in sleeping rough, many more would be sleeping rough than actually were found.

Thus, adding these figures together, we must accept the amazing fact that at least ten thousand people habitually or sometimes sleep rough in England, Scotland and Wales. It has been suggested that the figures given by the National Assistance Board researchers were far too low. For example, *The Observer* said, 'social workers and police officers think the total to be far higher than the Board suggests. . . . In Birmingham where the Board's total was 32, the Simon Community says there are at least 89. In Edinburgh, where the Board found 3, Simon Community workers found 55.'

Estimates of the number of people sleeping rough on any particular night vary a lot. The figure generally accepted seems to be; 4,000 on any one night; 2,000 of which are in London.

This is a figure for winter. It doesn't embrace the far larger number who sleep rough in summer when the nights are warm.

I'd like to speak now, in more detail, about the common lodging houses.

Common Lodging Houses are officially defined in the Public Health Act, 1936, as 'a house provided for the purpose of accommodating by night poor persons, not being members of the same family'. Colloquially, the description covers all similar places, whether officially registered as Common Lodging Houses or not.

David Brandon in *The Treadmill* (Christian Action pamphlet, 1969) says of Common Lodging Houses, 'These places have the structure and atmosphere of the old general mixed workhouses. They are mainly unselective. They are a wide variety of different places under one roof – old people's homes; chronic wards of the psychiatric hospitals; reception centres; and cheap hostels for the working man. . . .

'Change is not going to be easy. Any improvement in general facilities must ultimately mean a reduction in the total number of beds as it has in both the psychiatric hospitals and reception centres. The doss-houses must find more place for leisure facilities; personal belongings; privacy and interview rooms for social workers and medical staff. . . . At present lodging houses stand right outside the Welfare State.

Brandon also makes the point that the rejection goes two ways. These people have been rejected by society, but they have also rejected society.

The N.A.B. researchers found a total of 31,932 beds for men in common lodging houses and 2,664 beds for women of which about 5,730 were provided by Local Authorities, 8,000 by the Salvation Army, and 2,100 by the Church Army. Similar places are run by Rowton Houses, although unfortunately soon many of the Rowton Houses will be closed reducing the number of beds

58

available by thousands. At a lower level than the common lodging houses come the Reception Centres, colloquially known as 'Spikes'. You can stay there for a day or so provided you have no money. At the end of the war there were over three hundred, each a day's walk apart.

The National Assistance Act and later acts require the Supplementary Benefits Commission to make 'provision whereby persons without a settled way of life might be influenced to lead a more settled life'.

Local authorities have similar duties or powers; they have a duty to provide temporary accommodation to those whose homelessness 'could not reasonably have been foreseen, or in such other circumstances as the authority may in any particular case determine'. (National Assistance Act.) They have powers to build hostels for ex-inmates of psychiatric hospitals (Mental Health Act) and the State will undertake the cost of beds in hostels for ex-offenders (Criminal Justice Act).

Unfortunately the interpretation of their duties by both local authorities and the DHSS has been disappointing. Most of the Spikes have been closed.

Also, it is sad that the State has not been able to replace the thousands of beds lost through the closure of Rowton Houses. Friends in the DHSS tell me that a change in the law is required. At the moment they are only allowed to provide temporary accommodation, and, stretch this though they may, it doesn't allow them to replace permanent places which have closed. Accommodation is growing less. The number of those sleeping rough is rising.

The Spike may not always be the answer. In many of them the rules are so archaic and the atmosphere so brutal that people would rather sleep rough than go there. But that can be no excuse for having closed so many. They should have been adapted so that they became more suitable.

The N.A.B. researches found 1,896 men and sixty women using twenty-one Spikes in England, Scotland and Wales. This included forty-five women in London and five in Bradford, 148 men in Birmingham, 112 in Leicester, 100 in Brighton, and ninety-three in Wolverhampton. Most Spikes are administered by the Department of Health and Social Security, only four being still administered by the Local Authorities. The DHSS now has 2,066 beds and the Local Authorities 251. Improvements have recently taken place in some DHSS Spikes, and the intelligent involvement of this department indicates hope for the future.

I have seen round the renovated London Women's Spike, which is cosy but lacks that feeling of loving care that is a feature of, say, the Christian Action Hostels. Rehabilitation centres have been attached to DHSS Spikes. Many provincial Spikes are so full that the staff have to make the invidious choice as to who to keep in and who to ask to leave. As often happens, the kindly intentions of those at the top are sometimes weakened when they pass through the medium of staff who have been there for some time. Reports of appalling things being done to the inmates of some Spikes still come through to me. And my strongest feeling is still regret that, with so many thousands sleeping rough, so many Spikes have been closed.

The researchers also gave figures for the various types of people in Common Lodging Houses. A disturbing number had been in psychiatric hospital within the last two months. Twelve per cent of those interviewed were thought to be physically handicapped and 5 per cent mentally handicapped. About 21 per cent of those in Salvation Army Hostels were thought to be handicapped. About 28 per cent said they had been in prison and 3 per cent had been in prison within the last two months. Of those sleeping rough, 9.3 per cent said they had been in prison within the last two months, 6 per cent said they had been in hospital within the last two months. Of those in Spikes, 11.3 per cent were thought to be physically handicapped and 8.3 per cent mentally handicapped; 9 per cent had been in hospital in the last two months. Sixty per cent said they had been in prison and 9.4 per cent had been in prison within the last two months.

Recent research by the Salvation Army and Department of Social Security endorses this picture of an endless treadmill trudge, from nick to bin to Spike to kiphouse to doing a skipper to doing a job to returning to nick and so forth.

'I know a man who is doing life imprisonment at the moment because his own mother took him to court. . . . '

One of the earliest men to be aware that this vast population of thousands of people in the abyss in Britain, required more than just statutory justice, was the Welshman, Merfyn Turner.* He realised that they needed charity and, adults confined in many ways to the role of children, the only thing that really would help them was an artificial family which would replace the family they never had.

60

With his wife he runs a family-like hostel, Norman House, in North London.

'The differences between down and outs and others are not fundamental,' he says, 'but sickness and health and normality and abnormality are just shades of each other.

'Long term prisoners seem to have a history of social failure. If they were born into families they seem to have broken with their families, or their families have rejected them.'

He continues, 'The man whose mother took him to court because he was beyond control, that might be regarded as a praiseworthy act on the part of the mother who takes her own child, and society might say that mother was a good mother. Now they've moved into a new district, the people around them are nice people and they don't know about this criminality in the family. They dissociate themselves and I don't think they *can* dissociate, that chap at this moment is doing a life sentence.

'It's this history of failure, failure in the family, failure at school, that characterises the down and out. They never seem to have done anything which raised them a little above others in the class, or had just that extra proficiency at sport. I don't know if there is any connection at all, but I am amazed at the absence of even a sufficient degree of proficiency, enough to give a man self-respect. And this is what I believe. I cannot myself see any man coming out of prison a better man than when he went in. Chiefly, I think, because the prison environment is artificial. You can't teach a man or help a man to become a good citizen out of society, you can't teach a man responsibility or lead him into responsibility in the artificial prison environment. You can't teach him good habits of work when you require him to sew a few mail-bags for four hours a day.

'The prisoner's problems have only been refrigerated because of the abnormality of the setting, and when he comes out, unless we face up to his particular difficulty, he's going to go back to prison.

'You say to the man, Well look, this living at my hostel, you know, it isn't quite as simple and as good and as nice as you think it will be. In the first place you'll have to get up in the mornings, and straight away he says, Oh Guv, I'm fine at getting up in the mornings. Look at me now, I've been in here for two years, and so on. Then you say, Well, not only will you have to get up in the mornings, you'll have to go to work. Guv, that's no trouble to me, I don't care, I've been a good worker in the past. You may already know, perhaps, from what he's told you over the months that he's got a shocking work record in the past. Then you say to him, The other thing is if you go out on Friday night and get yourself drunk – Look Guv, I never get drunk. And you finish it by saying, And if you go to the dogs on a Saturday afternoon and blow it – Guv, I never, never make a bet. And you begin to wonder, you see, what such a virtuous gentleman is doing inside a prison, unless he happened to be the governor or one of the superior officers such as the chaplain. Now these chaps come to my hostel, and it's interesting that what you see so frequently is a contradiction of what they said to you in prison.

'The very man who said to you, Look Guv, I'm fine at getting up in the morning, if you didn't give him a good shake he'd be in bed till dinner time. The man who said to you, Look Guv, I've got a fine work record, on the second day he has called for his cards because the foreman has given him a ticking off.

'One of the problems we find is not in getting a man a job, but in getting him to stick to it. A man will call for his cards because somebody told him that on the next building site the bloke doing the same job is getting threepence an hour more. So he calls for his cards and goes for a job on the next site, and finds there's no job there. We got to the point at one stage of telling the chaps, Look, anybody who changes his work now without proper cause and reason changes his lodgings as well. In short, I think what the men said when they were inside was sincere, and truthful, but it had to be interpreted within its own setting, within its own climate. Prison refrigerates a man.

'One thing that used to impress me was the ex-prisoner in Norman House who used to give me his unopened wage packet every Friday night asking me to take the rent from that. I used to think that man was showing great virtue, until I eventually realized what he was really doing. So many of these men, it seems to me, in lodging houses, on the road, and in prisons, have never shouldered the responsibility that we shoulder in ordinary day to day living. They've been brought up in children's homes, orphanages, on pocket money. They've been in approved schools on pocket money. They've been in Borstal on pocket money. They've gone to the forces and they've had pocket money. They've gone to prison and they're given pocket money. The only money they've ever possessed has been pocket money, and therefore when they come to Norman House on a Friday night or a Thursday night with their wages, the first thing to do is to get rid of this alarming idea of adult *wages*, to give it away so that the rest is pocket money.

'In the spare moments at the hostel we talk prison. We talk

prison from morning till night, because, for one thing, prison is the one subject to which everybody can contribute. Prison is the one subject that every man feels, well, he knows something about it. There are so many other topics we can't discuss. The other point about talking prison is that society doesn't give offenders the opportunity to get rid of their aggression. Now a man who has been apprehended by the police, and who has been sentenced by a court, is, inevitably, embittered. He feels that all lawyers are crooked because his case failed. All policemen are crooked because he got done; all magistrates are crooked, and the whole of society is rotten. Yet the community doesn't give that man the chance of getting it off his chest. And it seems to me that until the man has got rid of that sort of aggression you can't begin to secure an adjustment, so that one of the first things that we offer is, simply, acceptance.

'Material help in itself is not sufficient. It is this emotional help, it is being related to somebody who is prepared to accept a chap for what he is. It's this, the presence of somebody who notices that a man has bought a shirt, and you say to him, Look you've got a parcel under your arm, what've you been buying? He says, I bought a shirt, do you want to see? You say, Yes, of course I want to see your shirt. It's being there to notice that a man has bought a shirt, if there's nobody there to notice, what point is there in buying it, it's much simpler to thieve it.

'That is what my place, I hope, gives to them. What it has come to give me is probably far more than any of the offenders who live at Norman House get out of it. I think one can never under-estimate (whether one is behaving as a professional social worker, voluntary worker, or as a private man who is giving a bit of help where it's needed) the amount of benefit that comes to *oneself* in the process of sharing somebody's troubles. This also goes for my wife, we have benefited considerably more from living and working at Norman House than we would from any other way of life. And I'm not saying it sentimentally when I say that many of the real friends we have at the present time are men who came to this place because they needed what the place had to give. The fact that we're still friends, I think, in active contact, does suggest at least that this process of helping is a two-way business, and that it is never a one-way business, a case of you giving something and asking nothing in return. Always the other person has some-thing to give to you. Prison visiting in particular teaches you this; and if it doesn't teach it, well, you shouldn't continue. The man in the cell has as much to give you as you have to give him.

'In Wales I did actually grow up in a tradition of helping people out. In this village where my father was minister you were always being asked to participate in efforts to help people overseas, then there were home missions, collections regularly, you never knew what they were for, you just knew their names. There was a London Mission, there was a West London Mission, there was and East End Mission.

'Now what sort of man is your criminal? There is a vast pool of men who are potential criminals, and they are the tens of thousands of men who are on the road or in the dosshouses. In my young days workhouses, as they were called then, were placed a day's walking distance apart. Living in a rural community in a village, there was nothing to interest children, except a few houses and the road. And this road led from one workhouse to another. And the tramps and dossers who left that particular workhouse in the morning, would very probably be passing through your village in the afternoon to get to the other workhouse by the evening. And you got to know them. And a tramp would tell you, So long now, I'll be back again in two or three weeks time. And in your own childlike way you would look forward to their coming, in a sense as you look forward to Father Christmas I suppose. We would look forward to these tramps therefore and walk with them out in the village, sit down beside the roadside, help them, or be allowed to help them, to light their fires. One particular man I remember used to let me comb his hair. One afternoon I brought a tramp up to our garden; we had visitors at the time, I could only have been about six. Bringing the tramp up to the front garden because we had visitors at the time, and one of the visitors had brought a camera. They were taking photographs, and I'd been asked to have my picture taken with the family, and I said to this old tramp, Come on up to our house, because we're having our photos taken and you must come, and he came and he said to my parents, Your little boy has brought me to have my picture taken! Well I suppose they considered that peculiar, but it's not peculiar, really. A child's judgement of goodness is different from an adult's.

'Now I'm not saying that every man on the road is a criminal, far from it. But the man on the road has been thrown away by society, sometimes he's on the run, but not very often. The Spikes and lodging houses where these men stay form a reservoir from which petty criminals spring. When you're starving you don't worry very much who the potatoes you steal really belong to.

'Now whatever a man who's on the road tells you, it seems to me even if he says, "Yes, I like the open road, it's freedom," that that man is confessing to himself that the open road is slavery. There is no freedom, there is no point, there is no ending. And there is no pleasure, there is no happiness, and I think it's we who read and romanticise what we read in books and so on who say, Ah yes, the freedom of the road. I was given a poem once by quite an intelligent, youngish man, he claimed to have spent many years on the road. "There's freedom," he said. He was saying that for him the road meant freedom, and he recited a poem which he claimed to have written himself.

I was never bitter, though my heart was sad,
For many broken friendships litter the road of life so hard,
Blow, savage winds, and bring the lashing rain,
There's a sweetness in her sorrows, and a glory in her pain,
I leave the dreary city, its artificial lights,
Away from the wiles of women and sensual delights,
I'll wander round the country free without a care,
I'll sit by dreaming streams and breathe deep of freedom's air.

'I was impressed, naturally, as anybody would have been impressed to hear the man reciting his poem. But if he wasn't being totally insincere, I would say that he is and was deluding himself absolutely, and that when he says, you see, "I leave the dreary city, its artificial lights, Away from the wiles of women and sensual delights," what he's really saying, if he's honest is, I want the artificial lights and the city and I want the women and the sensual delights, but it's my failure in that sphere that causes me to escape to the open road. And then he says, "I'll wander round the country free without a care". Well, he's wandering around the country all right, but he's taking all his cares with him, because he's got the worry that comes from escaping his problems and his responsibilities. And, "I'll sit by dreaming streams and breathe deep of freedom's air," sitting by dreaming streams is all right when the sun is shining and the sky is blue, when you've already had a good meal and you're enjoying a nice smoke, and what's more important, when you know where the next meal is coming from, and your next cup of tea. But that, in the life of so many road men, is not the pattern. They haven't had a meal today and they don't know whether they're going to have one tomorrow.

'I think the winter weather, the rain and the cold beats every man sooner or later. And however much he resists institutional care, sooner or later he'll arrive at an institution. He either commits a crime to take him into prison, or he arrives at the doors of the lodging house or reception centre or Spike.

'As far as these places are concerned, although men are not deprived of their liberty in lodging houses, in a social and economic sense I think they are truly deprived, and although we say, So-and-so booked in tonight with his own money, what we are really saying is that society has sent him there.

'He has the apparent freedom to walk out of the door, but really he has no freedom.'

A tall, gaunt, attractive man in huge grey flannels and a too tight white jersey, with an exotic, gaunt, saint's face, spoke in a lazy Somerset voice, 'When I was young I went to a number of foster homes, I believe I went to about seventeen homes before I was fifteen, the reason being my Mum found it hard to cope with all of us by herself. So she kept my brother at home, but she couldn't manage the others, so me and my sister went out to foster parents, and as I say, I had about seventeen changes before I was fifteen.

'Later I came up to London. And I was walking about on that first night in the park and I met a policeman, he said, "Where are you going at this time of night, it's time you were in bed." I said, "So I would be, only I have nowhere to go to bed. I thought I'd sleep out." So he gave me a tanner and he sent me down to the Spike in Gordon Road. I had my clothes defumigated and that, and I slept the night there, and the following morning they said, "You're new here aren't you, you'll have to see the officer." So then I don't know why, I really don't know why, but I climbed over the wall and got out. I walked around the streets all day and in the evening I went back to the park and lay down under four deckchairs, and I slept there quite well, till later that night a policeman came along and told me to get moving. So I did get moving and I walked about till the dawn. The next night after that I slept more concealed, under the bushes. And when I woke up there was a real old-fashioned tramp lying there on newspaper just beside me. We peered at each other, you know, but we didn't say anything. After a few days I began to get hungry and it was then I betook me to the road. I travelled the casual wards, and often in between I slept rough. I was ashamed to show myself. I had intended to go to farms to ask for work, but by now the hair had grown on me and I was ashamed.

'It was on the seventh day that I was hungry. I was passing through a town, and there was a newspaper stall lying unattended. On the counter of the newspaper stall was a plate with fivepence in it.

'So I looked around and there was no one watching, so I took the fivepence and a paper as well, and I suppose someone must have seen this because a little farther on a police car drew up and the copper looked out and asked if I had taken fivepence. So that's how I found myself inside, for thieving.'

How to turn the inadequate or even the just eccentric into a criminal or madman; our legal system, law, police, and welfare state can sometimes seem to be an essay in just that.

Colin McInnes has said, 'For ninety per cent of non-professional criminals there's little chance of cure in prison, indeed in a majority of cases the harm they would do to society were they not locked up is probably less than the harm they *will* do once they come out again'.

Every now and again an item like this appears in the newspaper:

MAN OF SIXTY-FOUR PREFERS PRISON

'Said to have told the police that he could not adjust himself to freedom, a man was sentenced at Middlesex Sessions yesterday.

'Charles William Perry, aged sixty-four, described as a labourer, of no fixed address, had been committed for sentence by the Enfield Magistrates after being convicted of attempted shopbreaking and possessing house-breaking implements by night.

'Detective Sergeant D. Gilder said Perry was seen by a policeman trying to break a plate glass window with a stone at a jeweller's shop in Enfield on March 25th only six days after he had been released from prison. When arrested Perry said that he wanted to be sent back to prison for a long time as he could not adjust himself to being free. He did not want to go to an old people's home.

' "Since 1927 Perry has been sentenced to terms of imprisonment totalling forty-nine years, four months," Detective Sergeant Gilder stated. Perry had a total of twenty-four convictions. "Since 1927 the longest period of liberty Perry has had was four months from October, 1955, to January, 1956,' the officer said.'

In a hostel for ex-prisoners in Southampton* I spoke to Tony, a young man who had been brought up by his mother. He had a twisted body and a turned up crooked nose and a look of perpetual surprise on his face. He'd grown up at Greys Thurrop, and from early on the West End and all that it represents has fascinated him.

Even as a boy he used to come up to the West End and peer in an astounded way at cars. at the girlie mags in shop windows, and, whenever he could afford it, go to striptease shows.

It was his way of looking at cars that got him in trouble. He would peer, astonished, into the interiors of Jaguars and Bentleys, particularly if there was inside them some object which awoke his interest, such as a fur rug or handbag or movie camera. Sometimes he would open the car doors, pick up the objects and finger them in astonishment. He had not grasped the concept of property. Indeed, so little was this concept developed in him that he would most likely have walked off with these intriguing things had it not been that his investigations were conducted with such openness, such complete lack of guile, that passers-by would see him and he would inevitably be taken in by the police.

On one occasion, astounded by the beauty of a car, he climbed in and sat at the wheel. Later it was revealed that this was a stolen car. Surrealist interrogation by the police ensued in which Tony was unable to remember where he lived. This was interpreted as lack of cooperation.

Tony had done various sentences before he was rescued by the hostel. No better example could be found of someone who, inadequate, was turned into a criminal. Soon after his arrival at the hostel it was discovered that he had not long to live.

Tony was a child of this age. He surrounded the bunk in the corner of his dormitory with glossy pin-ups of girls and motors. He listened to Pirate Radio and Radio Luxembourg. He desired above all to enter the world of fashionable young men, a world for which he was ill-equipped. Once when the warden was trying to encourage one of the inhabitants of the hostel to get himself a job, Tony up-ended his nose and asked, 'What about a job for me, warden?'

The warden said, 'You're all right, Tony, you've done well, you've broken your record of not getting work. You've actually had a job.'

'Yes, but it was only for half a day, warden.'

'Even so, Tony, you can be proud of yourself. At least you've had a job.'

Not so long after this he died.

Another man there has always lost job after job and this had been taken as an example of uncooperativeness. He had supplemented his periods of freedom with petty pilfering, and this in turn had resulted in his spending long periods in gaol.

Almost by chance the reason for his losing his job was discovered, he was partially deaf and had so little communication with the outside world that he didn't realise this.

Another man in the hostel was Bert, a strange looking person with a great livid scar across his face, who always spoke twice as fast as anyone else, and was consequently hard to understand. His incredible gabble was amazing. It is difficult to see how anyone could fail to realize that here was a man in need of help.

He had spent the greater part of his life in gaol.

A policeman told me, 'You can imagine what it's like for a lot of them, they've got used to it, it's as if you've been doing the same job for fifteen years and then you lose it, they turn you out. Obviously, in that situation, you feel absolutely lost. It's like that for a man when he gets out of gaol. He goes around one or two places to try to get a job and they turn him down because he's been in the nick, it's hard, he finds it too much, so then because he finds that the world's too hard, he nicks something. You get some, they find it so hard that the moment they get out they do two or three jobs.

'And some definitely do prefer to be inside rather than out. We had one the other day who'd been inside seventeen years in all, on nine charges, one for stealing milk bottles, four for throwing bricks through shop windows.'

The saddest of all the men I saw there was Charlie Portman, an epileptic character 'of low mentality' who was given ten years imprisonment for stealing a box of chocolates and twelve Bovril cubes. This was preventive detention after a long series of petty thefts.

The theft had not even been noticed until he reported it to the police a couple of months after he did it, in order, so he said, to get himself a roof over his head during December.

The warden was able to get the sentence deferred so he could be at the hostel. He wrote in a letter, 'This is the first time I got a nice place to live what I read in the papers.'

His mother was dead and he had never known a father. He couldn't keep straight. After a few weeks at the hostel he stole six pounds and returned to prison, when he wrote this letter.

My dear warden,
    My charg was stealing £6.
    I agree with the names you called me.
    I have got free Legal Aid.
    I deserve what I got becous I have let you Steve and Farther down a great lot by comming here.

I do not want to com back.

If Jill calls, tell her where I am.

I don't want ennybodies help inside or out.

I am in that state know the way I fell is I don't care about anything.

There is one thing I want you to know.

I was not born at Kensington London it was Holway Prison.

Good luck in the Coming days

Roll on ten years

A young man of twenty-four with a sallow complexion and a small, neat moustache said, 'I had a row with my mother when I was seventeen, that's how I started. Perhaps I was trying to get her attention. So I walked out of the place and when it got dark I hadn't got any money so I went round to the house of some friends of my parents and I did it. I did the place out. I got some money and some food. The police found out, and I got put on probation. But it's as if the taste for it had got me. I went on rowing with my mother and I went on stealing.

'Finally it came to the point that when I was next in court they said I couldn't go out unless I paid twenty-five pounds. And someone went ten pounds for me. I still needed fifteen pounds. So I said, "My mother's in court, ask her." They said, "Will you go bail for your son?"

'And my mother got up in court and said, "I have no son."

'I think they were all shocked, I was. I went into the nick after that and when I got out of the nick I went back to my home town and did a really big job this time, so big that I could be sure that my name got in the papers. It did. The family name *was* disgraced. I don't know why really, but I seemed to want to disgrace them. And when I came out next time, this was after three years, I got a rail warrant back home, and in spite of the fact that I think I'd half done it to shame them, now I seemed to want to go back there. So I went home and when I got there they slammed the door in my face. So there wasn't much I could do. I'd got a few bob in my pocket but not enough for the night. That's when you feel like doing a job again, and that's what I did, actually. That's the way I got started.'

Another man said, 'I was all right when I first came out of the nick, I got a job all right, it was fine except I didn't tell them I'd been inside, so one day some gear disappeared, and the law come around checking up because naturally their suspicions lighted on me, and so the firm got to know and out I went, you know, at the end of the week that's that, services no longer required.'

The warden said, 'That's the trouble with a lot of them here, they will not tell their employers the true situation. So when something happens and the boss gets to know, out they go. On the other hand, their instinct may well be correct. We fixed up a job for one of our men here the right way, with the appointments officer from a chain of booksellers. The man worked for a week or so. Then the appointments officer wrote to his firm's central office, he said it was just a formality, and the result was, Sorry, but it's a standing rule, we can't employ you.'

Another man at the hostel told me, 'It's true I did nick a few things when I was a kid, but I went straight for ten years after that. It was my wife got me round to it again. She wanted to have a good time. She used to want to dress up of an evening, go out, you know, have a crate of Babycham, that sort of thing. That's how I started again on breaking and entering. And once again I was caught. And when I was inside again, I wanted to go straight. And it was something a bit different the next time, because while I was inside a change came over my wife and she got so as one man could no longer satisfy her, she needed more than one man, I'm sorry, I wasn't enough for her. She got turfed out of her lodgings while I was inside, and she and my child went to a Hostel for the Homeless. When I come out I lived in the Spike. I used to walk to see her every night. I was in work at the Cumberland Hotel. But even during the day, unbeknown to me, she used to have men in, so I've been told.

'A benevolent peer, whose name I will not say, got us fixed up, in a flat in Twickenham.

'My wife had become a Catholic and this peer was one as well, so he wanted to get her fixed up. But my wife continued in her evil. Nothing it seemed would stop her now. It was an unhappy time for me, and she would taunt me about my being too dull. And so I got so I wanted to go back.'

'Do you mean back to crime, or back inside?'

He thought for a moment. 'Well, both. They both come to the same thing in the long run, don't they?'

One night recently Jim Horne was standing in the darkness on London's Embankment, preparing to hand out soup to some twenty down and outs who were sleeping on the seats in this particular section. The seats are along an asphalt path used during the daytime by pedestrians. Behind the seats is greenery. Jim Horne, standing there, was surprised to see a police vehicle ascend the curb on to the pedestrian path and drive along between the seats on which were the sleeping figures. The car drove slowly and as it did, police leaned from the door, prodding the sleeping down and outs in the face. Awakened thus suddenly, many of them showed marked signs of fear. Some sprang to their feet and stood in the wake of the car, others sat bewildered on the seats, wondering what this sudden violence in the middle of the night betokened.

On other occasions plastic bags filled with water have allegedly been thrown by police at down and outs and police cars, with headlights flashing, have forced down and outs standing on the Embankment, whether maimed or whole, to jump for their lives. Some of the things witnessed by Horne have been the subject of a police enquiry whose results have been kept secret. A more curious method could hardly be imagined for solving a nation's Down and Out problem.

I had noticed how many of those I met in the Down and Out world had been in psychiatric hospital.

I decided to learn more about this; and first brought back to my mind memories of friends of mine who had entered that lost world.

And first a young man who had inhabited a large studio. When I first came to London he used to let me sleep on a mattress on the floor. A gallery held an exhibition of his weird and beautiful paintings, and he was preparing for a second one.

Then fate decreed that his life as a sane individual was over. His father decided to discontinue the allowance he was paying him, and this may have precipitated his downfall. I don't know. He stopped paying the rent on his studio, and was evicted.

He lived with various friends for a while, but some desire for death or failure had gripped him.

He painted less, and when he did, it was with less permanent substances – boot polish, lipstick, mud, excrement, found their way on to his canvases.

But, more tragic still, this young man of great charm and beauty for some reason got the idea that he was not an artist but a pop-singer. Hour after hour he would sit at his friends' pianos or harmoniums, strumming out chords, singing in a high-pitched and unacceptable voice. His wanderings began then too, through those vast areas of London that lie South of the river. He shaved his head bare. He became more dirty, but he was the gentlest, sweetest of people, and it was still good to see him

72

although he'd begun to smell.

He would go off into wild bursts of cackling laughter. He didn't paint much now. Instead he endlessly walked up and down the London roads, one arm held in the air. When people asked him why he did this, he said, 'I've sworn I will hold my arm in the air until such time as I've made half a million pounds.'

He would get from one former friend a piece of bread, from another a cup of tea, and his daytime was spent in pacing round London to those houses where he knew he could get food. And the people who at one time had been glad to see him now found him unpleasant because he smelled too much, and his talk had become abusive.

He wrote down accounts of his wanderings on endless sheets of paper, interspersing these with drawings. In these, he referred to himself by the name of 'Shorts', possibly suggesting his desire to return to a childlike state.

A little later this mildest of men, wandering down the Kings Road, was accosted by a policewoman.

The policewoman misinterpreted his arm raised in the air. She believed this to be an attempt at assault. The next thing he knew was that he found himself in prison. This was only for a week, but when he came out, he had retreated further from the world. Soon after that he was admitted for the first time to a psychiatric hospital.

At one point he lived in a house in Fulham whose owners had bought it cheap and then put bunk beds in every room, for which they charged two pounds per head per week. In each room there were eight bunk beds so that each room produced sixteen pounds a week. There were six rooms in the house so that the total income of the house was ninety-six pounds a week, or five thousand pounds each year, the price that it had been bought for.

Such overcrowding was against the law, but when the local Health Inspector came round the inmates of the house and the proprietors alike combined to deceive him by dismantling most of the beds and hiding them in the attic. The inmates, during the inspection, would go out and then return and get the beds back down from the attic.

There are many ways that lead out of the world.

Rudolph, another friend of mine, was an upright man with the bold bearing of a cavalry officer. He'd once been married to an Argentinian heiress. He would still tell people sometimes that he possessed five thousand acres of fertile land in the Argentine.

His frequent home was a large mental institution in South

London.

Wandering along the endless corridors, up endless tortuous circuitous staircases, at length I found him in a ward known by the letters E3. On the way I had accosted various staff and asked the way to this ward but many had answered carelessly or given incomprehensible replies. The manner of the staff was authoritarian and contemptuous.

Eventually I entered his ward. Here, about sixty people occupied a vast T-shaped area subdivided by two partitions which turned one part into a dining room (red and yellow shiny topped tables), a lounge (chintz covered armchairs and Windsor chairs), and a dormitory with the sixty beds arranged in four lines.

Sad people stood around doing nothing or collapsed in deteriorated positions in chairs.

One man, hunched like a bird, gave hawk-like dives down towards bits of paper on the floor, bus tickets and the like, which he picked up, chattering to himself.

But where was Rudolph? At length I saw him. He was at the extreme end of the dormitory, in bed already, the only sleeper amid a sea of beds.

Later he killed himself.

A third person I knew also took the trip that leads out of the world. She was a beautiful girl. She was exotic. Before such things were fashionable she dressed in skin-tight clothes and short skirts. Her progress down the street would result in enthusiastic cat-calls and shouts from passing lorries and cars and she became fatally hooked on purple hearts that had been prescribed by her G.P. in order to calm her nerves.

At a time when four or five were considered a lot, she stepped up her consumption till it was in scores every day.

And in the end she died.

There are 170,000 people in psychiatric hospital beds in England alone.

A recent report by CARE* claimed that three out of five of them have no health problem, either psychiatric or physical, apart from their subnormality.

'They do not need to be shut away for life. They could live happily in sheltered communities and lead useful lives. The big trouble at present is that apart from hospital the mentally ill have nowhere else to go.

'Facilities for caring for the mentally ill have improved a great deal in recent times. But the need is for more alternative accommodation to hospital.

'More than thirty-six thousand people are wrongly shut up. Many are locked away in ugly ancient buildings condemned to an empty life of boredom. And as there is an acute shortage of staff to look after them it is small wonder that there has been recent evidence of cruelty to patients.'

In 1969 it was reported in a newspaper that a ten-year-old Blackpool boy had been locked up in a Mental Hospital's Male Adult Ward for five months because 'there was nowhere else in the country to keep him'.

A Sister was dismissed from Springfield Psychiatric Hospital because she refused to be responsible for an additional ward of about thirty patients, some of them dangerous.

She was in charge of a ward of forty-six patients and was assisted by a young Spanish trainee nurse. She said that she could not be responsible for both wards and could not leave the young girl alone in a ward.

Apparently, because of lack of staff, and particularly of trained staff, it had been difficult to control patients. Recently one had been found dead in the hospital grounds -- she had cut her wrists and had been lying there for some time. There had been other cases of this sort of thing.

Untrained nurses had to be given too much responsibility because of the lack of trained nurses. The turnover of staff was exceptionally high because of the nurses' dissatisfaction.

Miss Kathleen Daly, Regional Organiser of the Confederation of Health Service Employees, commented, 'The tragedy about this woman, who acted on the dictates of her conscience, is that she is one of the limited number of fully trained nurses in the hospital. I feel that they've got rid of a jolly good nurse for reasons which just will not hold water. Her attitude throughout was one of conscientiousness. She acted out of concern for the safety of the young girl trainee nurse.

'On this particular night there were only twelve ward sisters in charge of a total of twenty-five wards.'

The National Society for Mentally Handicapped Children conducted an enquiry into conditions in mental deficiency hospitals. A member of the society described conditions in many hospitals as 'shameful and sad. Our conscience is very uneasy about these conditions.'

A magistrate said she had seen sixty girls and young women at Chelmsley Hospital, Coleshill, near Birmingham, 'herded together' in one room measuring fifteen feet by twenty feet. They belonged, she said, to the 'legions of the lost'. In one building the girls had to walk along an open balcony from the bathroom to their dormitory. Many of the patients had never received a visitor.

Edna's eating habits when she first arrived in the Psychiatric Unit seemed extraordinary even to other patients. For instance, she claimed that she would eat nothing but fish. However, when fish was brought to her, often she would sweep the lot onto the floor.

After many efforts on the part of the staff she would ultimately pick her plate up off the floor, put the kipper back on it, and sit gazing at it for some minutes until the food was congealing and getting cold.

She'd then spoon the kipper into her mouth, She wouldn't eat anything else but fish. She said that she was being poisoned. She accused everyone of poisoning her. To anything which was placed on her plate she'd say, for instance, 'This isn't food. They're giving me snot out of their noses.' Then frequently she'd put the fish in her mug and spoon it out again, occasionally flipping pieces of fish across at other people who were sitting at the dining table.

She poured tea over other inmates. She'd get up very positively, and she'd go across with her cup of tea and very gently, very firmly, pour the contents of her tea-cup, which had quite a lot of leaves in it, straight over another patient's head.

She was having ECT treatment, and after six treatments, she appeared to be better orientated than she had been when she first arrived.

At the group meetings, which were meant to be a form of therapy, she began to talk quite intelligently about her brother and about a group of young men whom she said she had known in Durham in the coalfields.

It subsequently turned out that she'd never been to Durham, or anywhere near a coalfield. But she was beginning to take an interest in life and in other patients and she was very kindly if somebody else threw a fit of hysterics or cried during a group meeting.

When she first arrived she seemed as if she were completely without any human attributes at all. She had a stone-faced complexion and used to peer into the distance for hours on end, so much so that if one of the nurses lifted her out of her chair, her knees would still be suspended in a sitting posture.

And the staff used to have to carry her off to her room in that state.

She had a room to herself at the psychiatric hospital because none of the other female patients would share with her. Perhaps they were rather frightened of her because she had fits of temper.

Then, after being there for three months, she became a changed person.

She even went out and bought herself a wig. Her hair that had been grey and straggly and dirty when she first arrived now looked cleaner and tidier. Previously she'd refused to have people helping her to wash it because she insisted they were putting toothpaste on her hair.

Often she tried to leave hospital, and when she was prevented from doing so would turn round and with all her strength fight with the people who were trying to prevent her.

She was a voluntary patient, but probably if she had actually succeeded in leaving they would have made her a compulsory patient.

Her ability to communicate was impaired when she first came in. She was frightened of people. She accused everybody of either being poisoners or Nazis.

She was in fact Jewish and some people had the impression that she might have been in a prisoner of war camp during the war, but this again wasn't so. She had a sort of fierce fear and the intense terror of someone who has been under negation from a Nazi power.

She lived in a private world of her own and her fear was expressed in intense depressions during which she was unable to communicate at all. If you talked to her, she didn't hear. If you held on to her, she wouldn't even shake you free, unless she was angry, in which case she'd turn on you, fight, or scratch, or hit you. She had been prescribed anti-depressant drugs in the form of pills which they found it difficult to give her, because she'd clamp her mouth shut so tightly.

She'd stand up for hours and her legs would get swollen. Sometimes as a result of all her standing, her ankles would be so swollen that she'd have to spend days in bed.

Then when she was better she'd stand in the corridor preventing people from passing, saying, 'You're all lost, you're all lost.'

Occasionally she'd give people permission to leave the ward (although it was actually locked) and say, 'Oh, you're all right, you're recovered, you can go out into the world now.'

When the houseman first came in on one of his twice-weekly visits to the patients, he'd say something like, 'Good morning, Edna, how are you feeling today?', and he'd repeat the question several times. And she would probably reply, 'All right, thank you.'

And then he'd ask her about her feet and were they hurting her, and she'd reply only, 'I want to go, I want to go. They're all poisoning me,' and he'd say, 'I don't think that's true, Edna, we're doing our best to help you,' and she'd say, 'Can I go? Can I go?' 'Well, we'll talk about that tomorrow.'

It was always tomorrow. For her and for a number of other patients who wanted to get out.

He wouldn't reason with her, say things like, 'But you know that you've got nowhere to go,' because she wasn't in any state to understand that.

Then he'd ask her whether she'd been able to eat. These were the most important things in her day. And she'd say she was still eating nothing but fish because everything else was poisoned, and the people who were cooking it had been poisoning it.

Often there was a trolley brought round at each meal time with the food pre-prepared on it, and Edna would go out and check the containers of food to see what they were. Frequently, if a plate was put down in front of her, she would throw it on the floor or at the nurse who gave it to her, because she was frightened that she was being poisoned.

She was terrified of the other patients in the psychiatric hospital, and in some ways she was right to be.

In this ward there was a good chance that somebody would try to assault you sexually, and there was a good chance of a fight in those wards where people were the more sick, the more helpless, the more crazy.

The clothes they wore in some of the male wards were filthy, often the men went about with their cocks hanging out, and shirts hanging out behind, and it was not that difficult to reach a ward like this, you only had to be violent to one of the nurses and it's very easy to end up there.

Recently it was reported that a sane man had spent forty-five years in a mental institution. When he first went in, in 1913, doctors' reports said that he was imbecile, and for years after there was recorded no change.

But the man *could* understand, his hearing and understanding were perfect. It was just that he couldn't communicate with doctors.

At last he met the right doctor, and, after only twenty-four lessons, he was able to leave the institution, certified as normal and sane.

Here is the story of an apparently sane girl who, at the age of ten was, with her father's consent, given officially into the care and custody of a guardian.

She had been playing truant from school. She was high-spirited, wayward and backward. Although she had been blamed for some petty pilfering nothing had ever been proved against her. Her parents were appalled when they discovered that Mary was now in a mental home. She was sent to Rampton detention centre for mentally defective criminals. For seventeen years her family fought in vain for her release. She worked there as a domestic and was locked nightly into a dormitory with defective women

An appeal from her was heard by one of the Mental Health tribunals set up by the Ministry of Health to hear appeals against such unjustified detention.

When told of their decision that she should return to her mother, the girl broke down in a torrent of tears lasting five minutes, then recovered her composure and thanked the tribunal.

Many of her family at different times had made minor efforts to secure Mary's release but had always been told, 'She's not well enough yet. Perhaps soon.'

Her stay in psychiatric hospital had begun in an Exeter Hospital for mental defectives. Then she was transferred no one knows why, to Rampton. The only reason ever given was that she had tried to run away from the Exeter Hospital.

Her brother sought the aid of the National Council for Civil Liberties. They sent a representative to see Mary. He was a Nottingham Civil Servant, whose hobby is helping others, and he took a day from his summer holiday to go to Rampton.

He said, 'I found there a girl breaking her heart to get out and perfectly able to cope with normal home life. I was told that she was sometimes bad tempered, but so would I be if they locked me up in Rampton.

'She seemed to bear her parents no ill-will for having signed away her freedom when she was ten, and she wanted to return to them. She reads the newspapers in Rampton and what she kept asking me was why she, a girl who had never committed a crime, was locked up when so many criminals were out and about.

'I was so impressed by her goodness and sincerity that I was determined to get her out if I could.'

An ex-inmate of a psychiatric hospital told me of a friend of his called Leonard.

'Leonard was admitted through Casualty into the psychiatric ward, and he shambled in wearing an old gaberdine mackintosh and boots with holes in them, and small pieces of green paper stuffed into the toes to keep the rain out. He was angry and drunk; probably he'd been drinking meths.

'When he was admitted to the ward, he went round banging doors for three or four hours. Finally they gave him an intravenous injection to put him to sleep for the night.

'He woke up in an equally morose and bitter mood. He told the doctor he didn't want anything to do with him. He'd been sent from a common lodging house because "he wouldn't get up in the morning".

'He'd been picked up in the street. The following morning the doctor said that he didn't think that Len had anything psychiatrically wrong with him. And that anyway they couldn't do anything in that unit. But if he wanted to go to a large psychiatric hospital they would give him a letter of introduction.

'Len declined this and told him if they wanted to move him they'd have to get transport. They refused and finally had to use force to get him to leave the hospital. And he then shambled off.

'He told me a little bit about his life. He'd been a merchant seaman. He'd travelled the world. He'd been kicked about by too many people for too long and the Welfare State was only prepared to kick him too.

'When he tried to get social security or supplementary benefit, he was told that he had to have a fixed address. Addresses are costly.

'I remember his first words when he first woke up in psychiatric hospital. He woke up and said, "Fuck the bleeding world!"

'And then went on with a whole series of very ripe adjectives. Then he went back to sleep. Here was somebody clearly in need of help. Somebody very much more in need of help than half the people in that rather smug psychiatric unit. He was over sixty-five. But for some reason he couldn't prove his age, and therefore he hadn't been able to get his old age pension. And he had no birth certificate.

'He had no means of finding out how to get hold of a birth certificate and I told him that they had records at Somerset House and he said, "Yeah, but they charge you a bleeding five bob to get them, anyway they wouldn't let me in." Here was a man who was completely outcast by society. He stank. His hair was dishevelled and dirty and long, he knew his name but might find it hard to convince others of it. He had no identity.

80

'He said that during the war he'd never had a ration book. One of the reasons why he joined the Merchant Navy was because he wanted to eat, and this was the only time he'd fed properly in the whole of his sixty years.

'So he was thrown out. He headed on towards the big mental hospital they'd recommended to him.

'I believe that a middle-class alcoholic would have been treated differently because probably he would have been able to articulate much more easily.'

Prison; this is another place which figures all too often in the life of the Down and Out.

In all, there are about 30,000 of us in custody of the prison service in England and Wales at any one time.

These figures include 28,500 convicted prisoners, 708 convicted unsentenced, and 2,461 'trial and remand'.*

Let me tell now how one young man ended up in prison after having taken part in a demonstration. His account is tame compared to many that could have been found, but quite a number of interesting and important things emerge from it.

'To start with I felt that the students who were demonstrating were almost too militant in some ways. I felt that they were too hung up about Vietnam. I wasn't terribly concerned about it. I went to the demonstration out of curiosity rather than to participate in anything violent.

'The march was very peaceful, we found ourselves in the square.

'The front line of the demonstrators was throwing grass and weird things and basically harmless missiles.

'Some of the demonstrators had come prepared for battle, they had crash helmets, and I think they probably had some concealed weapons. But they were the ones who seemed to get away scot free. They seemed to fight their way out of everything. But some of the other people got tangled up in it who were not violent at all. The result was, the police charged up to the crowd and just broke in all over the place with truncheons flying.

'I was appalled early on at the sight of a woman running away from the crowd carrying a child, both were screaming and blood was streaming down her face.

'I felt angry, and I responded accordingly. Threw some missiles. Nothing terribly violent. For most of the demonstration I kept out of it. But towards the end, people were moving out to some mopping up operations. And most of the militant people seemed to have gone by then. And we'd formed a cordon and we were chanting. And we were peaceful. There was no fighting at all in this cordon. The police we were facing were pushing us back. We weren't resisting terribly strongly. The policeman opposite me lifted his knee rather sharply, assaulted me. Then I was dragged through the cordon. I was dragged through the cordon and ended up on the ground. When I was down I had a boot in my face. Then I was thrown in a wagon with a few other people. There were a couple with bleeding heads, and others injured in various ways, and we were driven off to the Western Central Police Station and kept there all night, thirteen in a cell. I don't suppose many people slept. There was no bedding. Before this happened of course I was charged, I was amazed that I was charged with assault, this was rather unbelievable. Still, I thought, "This can't happen in Britain and the truth will come out in court."

'I was very ignorant of court procedure.

'For breakfast we had half a cup of tea. The overcrowding in that cell was amazing.

'I had to see a doctor because of my eye, so I was in a separate room before I was taken back to the cell. And there was one very kindly policeman who seemed to care and brought me a couple of glasses of water and asked me if I wanted anything else. But the rest of them were very antagonistic.

'And then when the morning came one of the sergeants there asked me if I wanted legal aid and this is not what I was expecting, and I said "No", and he said, "All right".

'Almost as soon as I stepped into court I found that a copper was giving evidence against me, and this copper was the one who charged me in the cell in Western Central the previous night, but I never saw him at the demonstration.

'The copper gave his evidence. It seemed a bit ridiculous. I realized I was on trial. I was speaking to the policeman sitting beside me asking him to tell me what was going on, "Why are they starting the trial now," and he told me to shut up.

'So I realised I had to defend myself there and then. I noticed that magistrate, policeman, and the police prosecution were firing questions at me, at least, that's the impression I got.

'The policeman said that I kicked through the police cordon, dived through the air and fisted him in the face. He had a little red bruise on one of his eyes. I pointed out this could have come at any time during the demonstration. I also pointed out that the policemen standing behind the cordon row were three yards behind. I couldn't kick through a distance of three yards. This didn't seem to matter to the magistrate or anybody else. And then the magistrate asked the clerk what was known about me. And he said that I was unemployed and of no fixed address.

'I was unemployed, but I had a fixed address at West Hampstead which I had given, so this was a lie. And the magistrate said, "Thirty days." It was pretty horrifying. I was trudged off to the cell. This is the one time when I did fight back. I was just struggling and shoving. And then I was put in a cell.

'And a bit later I was put in a Black Maria and transported to Brixton Prison.

'Once I got into the cell, there were some young guys from London there who'd had a life of stealing, thieving and Borstal. They were very, very friendly, very intelligent, and on my side in a way. They seemed to be nice characters, brought up in the East End, I think. And had just got involved in petty thieving, crime. One of them had just got married and his wife was expecting a baby, and so he was a bit sad about ending up inside again.

'Next morning I was detailed with other guys to scrub the whole wing through from end to end. And I got on well. And I could see the screws were rather surprised to see I was working so well. They were hoping that I would be idle. To be idle so they could push me.

'We were entitled to go to classes twice a week. We had a list of eight classes. There were a couple which I was interested in. But I wasn't allowed to choose. I was detailed to the first aid class and the choir. I can't sing.

'One week my job was to clean round the medical wing, they called it F Wing, and this was the most horrible thing I had to do there. They bring people here, as far as I could see, who are out of their minds. On this occasion there was some sort of briefing session going on with the screws, and the prisoner just got up, started walking away. He clearly just wasn't with it at all.

'So one of the screws went after him and brought him back and beat him up then and there. But he hadn't committed a crime, he obviously didn't know where he was or what he was doing at all.

'Another thing I remember was a junkie who was coming off heroin in a cell, the incredible screams of the man left there without any help, to withdraw from it on his own. It was a terrible thing and upset me no end. He was in a strait jacket.

'The screws are not pleasant. They find something in your background and then they go on and on needling you and needling you about it, making you feel really small.

'You feel very much at the mercy of these people, who you

know if they wanted to could get you back inside for months again.

'One day as I was having my lunch the screws came up and said, "Come on, you're going back to court."

'So I said, "What's going on?"

'But they just said, "Further charges."

'So down I went to reception and put my proper clothes back on, and then I was handcuffed and what had happened was that this left wing organisation had put some form of appeal through for me. But the screws didn't let me know that.

'And that seemed to me so mean, why build up needless uneasiness in me about this, when I finally got to court I was in such a state of nerves that I couldn't understand that what was actually happening was an appeal.'

An inquiry was ordered into a businessman's claim that he was beaten up by two prison officers and pushed down a flight of stairs in a jail.

The businessman said that he was punched repeatedly in the face and stomach. He said he was given a black eye and a tooth was knocked out.

The man had been sentenced to seven days in Winson Green Prison, Birmingham, for failing to pay rates on his offices in the city centre.

Then, the man alleged that he was refused permission to telephone his wife to arrange for the debt to be paid, and pushed downstairs and attacked by two prison officers.

A man was charged with entering a house and stealing property worth twenty-eight shillings and as a result of this was kept in prison for eleven weeks on remand.* Finally he was granted bail.

The judge said on this occasion, 'I have never come across a case with such a lack of a sense of proportion. The man has no previous convictions and he probably would not have been sent to prison anyway.'

The sort of needlessly hateful atmosphere that can obtain in a prison and affect even those who are innocent, was well described in the following letter to *The Times*.

Sir,

For the first time in my life I attempted to visit a man being held on remand in Brixton Prison recently. I took the precaution of telephoning the prison before my visit to inquire about arrangements, and was told that remand prisoners might receive visitors between 10.0 a.m. and 11.30 a.m. in the morning and 1.30 p.m. and 3.30 p.m. in the afternoon. Each prisoner was restricted to one set of visitors a day, but the prison authorities were unable to tell me whether my friend had been visited during the morning session.

Hoping that he had not, but being unable to visit during the morning, I set out at 12.30 p.m. to drive from my house in North West London all the way across the centre and South of the city with another friend who also wanted to see our mutual acquaintance.

At the prison we queued for 25 minutes before being told that the record book showed that our friend had in fact already received a visit that morning. We were obliged to spend 45 minutes driving back across London, making a total of three-man-hours totally fruitless travel in all.

Why is it not possible for a copy of the visit record book to be made available for checking by telephone?

But the fatuity of the situation was heightened by the attitude of the prison officer running the prison's 'Food Room' (where some articles may be left for the inmates by their visitors) and by the set of rules, or lack of them, to which he appeared to work. Forty cigarettes and a magazine, both as I discovered obtainable within the prison, were accepted on behalf of my friend. But my main offering, an 'automatic' bridge game, consisting of a board and printed sheets of card on which an individual can play a bridge hand against himself (and which certainly could not be bought at the prison shop) was turned down out of hand.

I had taken the game since my friend had complained strongly in a letter of the boredom of being on remand in prison and banned from working, and because he is a keen bridge player, normally. The 'automatic' game can only be played by one person.

The prison officer took one glance at the box containing the game and declared, 'Oo, he can't have that.' I asked why not. 'Well it's got cards in it for a start, and they are strictly banned.' I pointed out that there was not a single playing card in the box, and opened the lid to show him. 'Well, he still can't have it, it's a game.'

Somewhat surprised I asked if all games were banned to men who were as yet innocent citizens awaiting trial. 'Not necessarily.' So what was the rule? 'Well now, you bring something in, you see, and I say, No. So next time perhaps you bring

85

something different and maybe I'll say yes . . . or maybe I'll say no again. See?' (Cheery grin.)

Is it not punishment enough to be gaoled without trial? What conceivable reason is there for depriving a man of a solitaire bridge game, not to mention visitors? Is there some rational explanation which escapes me?

Whether we believe everything we are told about prison or not, the fact is that most men emerge from it angrier towards society than they were when they went in.

And this is dangerous for society because it creates a group of people who would like to destroy society.

The senselessness and expense to the public of shutting many of those that we do in vast institutions was well shown in Tom Clayton's *Men in Prison*.* A prisoner, formerly a stockbroker, told him, 'I'll give you a few thoughts on the nick. You should ask if sending me to prison for all these years did anybody any good? I slipped. Very well, I had to be punished. One could say that losing my professional good name was a punishment but I won't. The fact is that it cost at least £2,500 to punish me. Wouldn't it have been possible to give me a rugged twelve months in a nick like Pentonville, then some years weekend imprisonment beginning with every weekend for a year or two, then tapering off to once a month. I could have been earning my own keep through all those years. . . . They simply haven't begun to think. "You have sinned and therefore you will go to prison for several years," they say, and everybody is satisfied. They are punishing your family as much as they are punishing you. . . . All right, all right, I've heard the argument that society has to express its disapproval of crime through the sentences it imposes in its courts. I am not questioning all that. But don't you think it's like the doctor giving the same cure for every ailment? Somebody knocks an old lady over the head and runs away with her handbag – give him a dose of prison. Somebody cooks the books – the same dose of prison. . . . Don't you think we're trying to deal with a rather mixed-up situation too simply, old boy?'

Even if we feel that what happens to some particular man or type of man in prison is right, we must remember his womenfolk and children who are also punished. A report by National Lifeline revealed that a girl aged three spent a lot of her time searching in cupboards, and opening doors 'looking for Daddy'. The girl's mother had found it impossible to tell her that her father was in prison. The same secret, they said, had been kept from a fourteen-year-old boy and he became a professional shop-lifter.

The report said that there were 15,000 married men in Britain's prisons at any one time. And that an average of one third of the marriages broke up.

Boys especially turned to crime because of the absence of the father in prison. Although the child could be led to crime for other reasons, the father's sentence was seen as a main factor for anti-social feelings.

The report called for more co-operation from police when a man was arrested. 'Sometimes the woman may have no warning that her husband has been arrested. She can be frantic, going from one police station to another in search of him.' The report added that many prisons still restrict visits to thirty minutes a month.

A letter to *The Times* from Sir Alec Clegg concerned the effect on children of an insecure home background. A Q.C. had said that 50 per cent of offenders, he thought, came from such homes. Sir Alec wrote to the heads of nine institutions – prisons, Borstals, and Approved Schools – to ask if they confirmed this view. Five did, three said his figure was an underestimate, one was uncertain.

He commented:

We have surely to think hard about some of the things we do to children. Consider for instance this case. Mother deserts father and leaves him with four small children to look after. He gets into debt and as he does not pay for his electricity it is cut off. He reconnects it illegally and as it is his second offence he is given a nine months' sentence. Keeping him in jail and looking after his children while he is there probably costs the public somewhat over £1,500 and his electricity bill is paid for him when he comes out.

If someone asked me what is the best way of promoting delinquency in a child I should say that there is no certain recipe as it depends on the resilience of the child himself, but one of the most reliable methods I know is to get the mother to desert and put the father in gaol.

The question to which I should like an answer from people who are wise, knowledgeable, and experienced in these matters, is whether it is sensible to spend one thousand five hundred pounds of public money putting four children at risk, and if it is not what ought to be done in cases like this?

Again and again a person who follows current events with even a slight show of attention may sometimes wonder at strange things that go on. Rosie, for instance, the 'penniless tramp with a wealth of friends', who was well known in Soho for the singing and dancing he used to do in the street and the flowers that he wore on his clothes and behind his ears, was given a loving funeral. He was described in this way by a fruit stall holder: 'He was an incredibly kind man and well loved by everyone. His endless kindness especially to children made him a very popular figure.' A restaurant manageress said: 'He seemed to radiate happiness even though he was in incessant trouble with the police for drunkenness.'

Despite the rigours of a life lived much of the time in the open, despite the fact that he had lived through the winter of 1969 and survived to the spring, Rosie died at the early age of fifty-four. Why did he die? All we know is that he was offered the alternative of paying a fine or going to Brixton prison for drunkenness. He went to prison and there died. What a life in the open in the British winter could not do for him, prison achieved.

Let me now pass to a consideration of our law courts. One million seven hundred thousand of us are proceeded against each year in England and Wales in magistrates courts. Of these, 26,000 go on to other courts.

One day I heard that the Exploding Galaxy Exploratory Dance Group were to be in court.

I think perhaps one of the worst days I ever spent was at this trial. They were a group who were being persecuted, only, as far as I could see, because they wore unusual clothes and lived unusual lives.

I had been struck, when I visited their communal house in Balls Pond Road, London, by a quality of joy and innocence in them. But a sudden and unexpected visit from the police early in the morning put an end to all this, and it was followed by vicious attacks on the group in various newspapers.

This idealistic band of innocents found themselves branded in one newspaper as follows, 'So help me, here's another bunch of scruffy, long-haired, unwashed layabouts who believe they have solved all life's problems.'

Later, cannabis was found on premises where they were rehearsing – although the leader of the group was against the use of all stimulants, had turned people out of his house for using hash, and had a notice on the wall forbidding it. Police 'found' four packets of hash in this place but the Exploding Galaxy said it had been planted.

The case was taken through a couple of courts, and, in the second court, the decisions of the first were reversed.

Basically, the Exploding Galaxy achieved justice for themselves. All except one of them got off.

But on another level they had been destroyed. Neighbours had taken to lobbing stones through the windows of their house. Other neighbours would stop them in the street and ask where were the 'communal girls'. Hostility in the neighbourhood grew to such proportions that the Galaxy felt they had had enough.

After this somewhat nasty experience of British justice they disbanded all over the world. The Exploding Galaxy is no more.

Justice in its old-fashioned sense does not seem to be at the moment readily available to such minority groups as those who run off-beat journals, homosexuals, and those taking part in protest marches.

If we say that every citizen in Britain has the right to defend himself in court, we may forget sometimes the sheer agony and expense, both mental and financial, of defending a case; the awesomeness, the awfulness, the sheer disgustingness, of many British law courts.

For the uneducated, especially, the impending court case has a horror all its own, counting the days, the sleepless nights, before the final humiliation in front of the rejecting father figures.

It should be remembered that the court proceedings are not meant to be part of the punishment. After all a man may be innocent.

Do the courts and their sentences really deter from 'crime'? What is crime? Do they set about in any reliable way the task of preventing it? Or does their behaviour help to swell the ranks of those who are vicious or in despair?

A magistrate tells me, 'So often, people who have got into a mess from which they may or may not need help to extricate themselves, are quite unreasonably dragged through the courts. And every now and again one comes up against a piece of apparently pure mean-mindedness, the actual creation of crime by the police in order to secure a conviction.

'This should not be viewed with too much condemnation either. The police are after all paid by us to stamp out crime, and the simplest way to do this may well appear, to an unsophisticated policeman, to get as many convictions as possible even though some of the crimes may not be of a very genuine nature.'

Also, it has often been said that policemen are promoted according to the number of convictions that they can get.

On the occasion when we (the one out of forty citizens per year) come up against the law-givers whom we subsidise, is the impression they make on us a good one? Is the progress of justice marked with fairness and humanity? Or is it callous and blind, just like the bold, naked woman in whose guise justice used to be depicted?

The warden of a hostel told me, 'So often magistrates seem to look on the courts as a God-given opportunity to air their own patronage, to compensate for their own feelings of inadequacy, and to demonstrate their lack of any true feeling for the humanity of those who pass before them. And if this is so of magistrates and judges, it may be doubly true of solicitors and police.

'Often, I feel, both magistrates and judges reveal a remarkable lack of any real thinking about their roles and what they are trying to achieve apart from their own ego scenes.'

To see how we ordinary citizens are treated by those to whom we have granted the power of law givers, I thought it would be interesting to visit the courts as an observer.

Among many things that I noticed then, I will mention the following: a woman allegedly had been found by the police in a drunken state in the street. Apparently, according to the police, in the police station she had struck a police constable across the right eye and across his nose with her forearm, and had shouted, 'I'll tell you what you are, a fucking cunt.' But she could remember nothing of this. She was too drunk. Did it really happen? Did the police invent it? Or did they so rig things that they provoked her to the point that she struck them, thus getting a graver conviction?

So often it seems to me that the police, indeed the courts as a whole, are engaged in some tragic game. The pawns are ordinary citizens. The name of the game is, 'Now I've got you, you son of a bitch.'

A man who had spent much of his life in prison was called. Institutionalised to the point that life was probably very hard outside, it was being claimed that he was an incorrigible rogue. He had come out of prison after many years spent there. At his release he had four pounds on him. He came to London and got a job as scene shifter at the London Palladium. But when his employers learnt he'd been in prison they didn't require his services any longer, said the police.

But by what means did his employers learn that he had been inside? Who had told them, was it the police themselves?

He explained in court, 'My first prison sentence was for four years at the age of twenty-one. Since then I've never been given a chance or even given bail. I had nowhere to go, no job, four pounds in my pocket. I was honest. The first place I went to I said I have been in gaol and they wouldn't employ me: I tried one or two other places with the same result. At the next place I lied and I did get the job. I thought I was doing all right. Then someone told my employers. I was thrown out. I've never been given a chance, never.'

But the magistrate was unmoved by this appeal. 'This is non-sense. Many people along the line have tried to help you.' And he found him guilty.

'Do you wish to apply for legal aid?' he asked.

'No.'

'If you wish to have bail you can apply.' He told him where to apply.

'I do not,' said the man.

There was a strange smile on his face. He had been conquered by the State. And he was not fighting back any more.

Insight into the mind of Sir John Waldron, until recently Chief of Scotland Yard, was afforded by the following speech:

'This is the age of permissiveness . . . the age of fiddling.

'This is the age of everyone living up to the hilt, with little pride in honesty, and no stigma if you appear in court.

'There is an attitude of "What can I get away with?" And we all know that the stolen lorry loaded with goods like food and whisky can have its goods sold at cut price almost before it is stolen.

'There has been a great lowering of moral standards.'

Sir John was talking of the factors that had led to a 22,564 jump in serious crime in the Metropolitan Police District.

These words of his are indeed impressive words. But are they the right words?

Is this really the most sophisticated attitude that a Chief of police could have to the increase in crime? I don't know.

Is it rather like a doctor saying, 'We live in an age of disease! Germs are everywhere and they don't care what they do. Germs have no standards these days. This is the age of germs.'

If the disease rate started rising uncontrollably now, I feel doctors wouldn't say that. Surely they would say, 'These germs seem to be getting a hold. We must be doing something wrong.'

If there's been an increase in crime and violence the blame may lie in us. Why, with the best technology in the world, in one of the richest countries in the world, are there still crimes of violence? What *is* our civilisation? Is it a civilisation at all if it's producing *that*?

An attractive girl sits on the sofa in her pleasant council house living room, in a Welsh town. Her two children are playing on the floor at her feet.

It is a dimmity scene. Yet this girl has just been convicted of keeping a brothel.

She tells me, 'My husband left me but since then I've been having quite a good time really. We used to have these parties you know. But other people on the estate began to complain. They didn't like to see so much happiness, or something.

'Then the police started snooping.

'We used to have these all night parties, and the boys and girls used to sleep with one another, sometimes we'd go upstairs and have sex.

'We used to get some drink in and have a great time drinking and petting, you know, and having sex. Young kids used to come that hadn't anywhere else to go to make love. This is a new town and life here can get a bit bleak.

'Then the police came. It was after midnight, and I was in bed.

'People had been coming up every now and again to talk to me and see was I all right.

'A policeman saw this through a curtain and thought it very sinister I suppose.

'My boy-friend was in bed with me when the police came. Two of the other boys were in bed with two other girls.

'Three other boys were downstairs and two of them were asleep.

'It was just an example of communal sex, not very sinister. But this is not what the law thought. I don't think they really thought we were running a brothel, but they thought that with us having such a good time there must be something a bit rum or immoral, anyway they thought they could get a conviction, and that leads to promotion.

'So they invented some pretty little story how they'd heard money changing hands. One of the policemen was peering through the front room curtains and he managed to hear and see a remarkable number of things through them. He said he heard sounds of people getting into bed, and that he'd heard a girl say,

"You'll pay me next time," and also heard the clink of coins.

'Anyway, they found me guilty of keeping a brothel, and the magistrate, drawing himself up solemnly said, something like, His colleagues and him take a very serious view of the incident seeing that boys and girls of fifteen, sixteen and seventeen were involved.

'But what's all the fuss about except that my name has been blackened through the town. What's all the fuss? We were just having fun. And, isn't it good for boys and girls of that age to get a taste of sex?'

It is quite possible, of course, that these kids *were* giving each other money.

But, even if they were, was dragging them through a magistrate's court really an appropriate reaction on the part of the State?

If the State really thinks it is wrong for youngsters to have sex, or even pay for it, surely we should allot people to help them and advise them, rather than drag them through the courts?

Just as the brutality of prison rubs off also onto those who are merely on remand or visiting, so the pompous rancour and violence of the court is not confined to those who are guilty.

A fourteen-year-old girl who had run away from Remand Home to live with her lover was described by Justice Seaton as a 'young huzzy'. And this girl wasn't accused of any crime, she was just one of the witnesses.

What a terrible thing that is, it seems to me, for a mature man to say about a young girl, in front of a crowded court.

It would be utterly understandable for that schoolgirl, smarting under a description like that from a man whom she might well regard as a father figure, to turn against a society that was so unfriendly towards her.

Surely *this* is not the way to turn a misguided young person into a reasonable citizen? Can it be that the man has no awareness that that way criminals are made? That *that* is the way to despair?

Does our system of punishment deter from crime, or does it perhaps create that very criminal mentality, that orientation to failure, which it was designed to stamp out?

Are those who administer our law inspired by that humanity and compassion which must be the hallmark of the just society? Or are they sometimes the victims of their own vindictiveness and other sadder things?

A lady made an anonymous call to the police to say that a neighbour of hers had 'got rid' of a child. She alleged that she was the mother of a ten-day-old child, that she had taken it to a neighbour to get rid of it. She said she'd changed her mind and wanted it back, then discovered that her neighbour had disposed of it in a suitcase. 'I saw my baby's clothes in her dustbin.'

The constable that took the call asked for her name and address, but she refused to give it and rang off.

Obviously this had to be followed up by the police because it was an allegation of murder.

But I wonder whether it was necessary, when her story was found to be the fabrication of this lady's sick mind, that this woman with her pathetic aberration had to be dragged through the courts, with the resultant newspaper publicity.

Her defence said, 'This is a lady of impeccable character and obviously this is a medical and not a criminal case. She suffers from blackouts and cannot remember making these phone calls although she admits that she must have done so. The trouble took place at a time when she had a severe medical illness.'

She was convicted of, 'causing wasteful employment of the police'. A total of forty-one hours in fact, or less than one man's week.

She was committed to much suffering, by the appalling pain caused her through publicity in the small town where she lived.

How can the loss of one man's week possibly justify putting this person, already mentally sick, through the horror of a court and all its resultant publicity? Was the 'full panoply of the law' designed for this?

It was night time in a ship on the Mersey. There was music and wine. A Swedish Lieutenant, long starved of female company, found he was enjoying himself. And when one of the girls revealed that she was 'adrift from the shore' he offered to put her up for the night.

The girl went back in the morning to the Liverpool street where she lived. It was 10 a.m., and she found her three little children just about to be taken off into care.

Later, she was sent to prison for three months for her neglect of them.

Even if it was right that she should be imprisoned for what was an irresponsible act, was what happened really fair on the children?

They needed their mother and she had been neglecting them.

And the punishment she was given perpetrated the very thing that it was meant to cure. If the aim is to prevent the mother spending a night away from her children, then it seems an odd way to go about it to force her to spend one hundred nights away from her children.

Her husband had left her, and, as her defence put it, 'Life had grown out of all proportion for her.' So, was not he a guilty party? Ought not he too to be punished?

A member of a family charity wrote to me, 'There is no question of course, that she *was* neglecting her children and that action needed to be taken.

'I asked for more details because I felt that to sentence such a mother to prison was a quite inappropriate way of dealing with someone whose real offence was that she had become quite unable to cope, or put her children's need before her own.

'My enquiries revealed that she had been in the care of the local authority from the age of eight, and passed through twenty-one different foster homes.

'The insecurity took its toll of her and she had an illegitimate child at the age of sixteen. Then her husband deserted her and she attempted suicide.

'This story brings home to me many things, the inappropriateness of the sentence, the repetition of the same details from one generation to another, the interweaving of childhood deprivation, disturbed relationships, depression, neglect of herself and of others.'

And so we reach the question of human responsibility. A person can be so battered and institutionalised that they are not really responsible for what they do.

Insecurity and inadequacy take place on an epic scale. Behaviour patterns established in one generation are repeated through the next and the next. Mental sickness takes place on a proscenium that is epic in its proportions.

And, if this woman behaved in this irresponsible way, does not the responsibility rest with Liverpool itself, that Liverpool which put her through such an unnecessary and insecure-making number of foster homes.

Is it not irresponsible for that Local Authority, having created, or at least contributed to behaviour patterns like hers, to then turn round and play the 'holier than thou' game?

A Welshman had a wife called Lola, and a mistress called Maureen. One day he told the mistress that he didn't want to see her again. Later she made a phone call in which she said, if he didn't see her again she'd tell his wife.

The man, upset and confused by this, after having spent the evening drinking, went round to the house of his mistress and talked to her mother. Apparently he threatened to 'fix Maureen', and refused to go away, presumably because he was terrified about the outcome of Maureen telling his wife.

Maureen's mother rang for the police and the situation was further complicated by the arrival of Maureen and her new boyfriend in a car.

What happened after that seems somewhat confused. When it came to court the man admitted he had been drunk and said he had been annoyed by the form of the police questioning and that a 'bit of a struggle' followed. In the confusion various people had a bash at each other, and he was later surprised to be charged with 'assaulting P.C. Jones in the execution of his duty, using threatening, abusive and insulting words likely to cause a breach of the peace, and with causing Maureen actual bodily harm'.

Was it really necessary for this rather sordid little affair to come to the courts?

Anyway, who is really the victim of this little story? Is it the man, because he took on a wife and a mistress in the first place? Is it Maureen for consorting with a married man and then trying to blackmail him? Is it Maureen's mother for calling in the police or is it the police for creating an incident that, as far as I can see, would have been more peaceable had they not been around?

The police alleged that the man attacked Maureen after she got out of her boy-friend's car, but under cross examination it was admitted that it was possible that he had slipped and collided with her without intending to attack her. This charge was dismissed in court and the only charges that he was found guilty of concerned his attitude to the police.

What if the police had not arrived in the first place?

And, was he justified in swearing at them? And, once he had done so, was it really necessary to take this case to court?

Above all, was it necessary that through all this publicity his wife was not only informed of what was going on but also humiliated in front of her friends?

A boy of nineteen was taken to court for having intercourse with a girl of fifteen. He admitted that he had had intercourse with her, and refused to promise not to see her. But he was prepared to marry her. He was sent to prison.

A fourteen-year-old girl was considered beyond the control of her parents because she had been 'subject to sexual offences'. She was put in the care of a probation officer and for some months her behaviour was 'reasonably satisfactory' until she again became a source of considerable concern. The probation officer brought her before the court, 'in her own interest'.

He said that she had been 'associating with local people and taking more notice of them than her mother'. And that three times, including the night before the court, she was out all night. The girl was sent to a Remand Centre.

But does society do right to shut up girls for behaviour which, if they were a little older, might be considered unusual but certainly not illegal?

The recent Home Secretary, Mr Henry Brooke, said a short time ago, 'Now that many moral restrictions of the past seem to have disappeared there is a real problem of how to deal with some young girls expecting babies.

'We all have to accept that difficult girls are more difficult than difficult boys, and we don't yet know how to handle them in this affluent and freedom-seeking society.

'These girls may be impossible to handle in a very small school. It is better that they should be in a large school run on the house or group system.'*

He was however criticised by Alice Bacon, M.P., who said, 'If we are going to shut up every teenage girl who might become pregnant, then the Secretary will have to provide a good many more approved schools.

'Every parent of a teenage daughter has the fear at some time or another that the girl is going to get into trouble. It is monstrous that girls should be shut up in this way.'

The law takes almost no account of the mental age of young people, as opposed to their physical age.

It is a criminal offence to have intercourse with a minor, so that there has sometimes been the pathetic situation of a boy and girl of fifteen who are in love and who want to get married (but who can't because marriage is illegal before the age of sixteen) being taken through the courts, and separated from each other.

A twenty-nine-year-old man fell in love with a girl of fifteen. He was a married man with two children and the girl's parents and his family tried to put an end to the friendship. The man was to be taken to court because of his 'association' with the girl.

We can only guess at the heartbreak that they must both have felt from the fact that these two killed themselves, dying in a car filled with exhaust fumes.

Was this an appropriate response on the part of the State to the man's situation? Was it a just response?

I imagine that, in thinking it over, he realised that the matter would be in the newspapers so that his wife would inevitably find out and be caused pain, and that he would face prison. The girl would be in danger of being sent to an Approved School.

Was all this necessary? Can it be that a girl of fifteen is possibly mature enough to know her own mind? Is she in greater danger as a result of being exploited by a man than she is of being broken up by a stay in a reformatory institution?

Sometimes, I'm sad to say, the Press joins in the hounding of people.

A DEN OF VICE IN EXCLUSIVE W.1 screams a headline. Brothels, as I understand them, are necessary to our society. They are almost as necessary a service as the social security. Where the one provides money for those who are short of it in hygienic yet somewhat humiliating circumstances, the other does the same with sex.

Some people, not well endowed, may find it hard to get sex yet need it. For them the brothel is vital.

There are countries like Germany where brothels are congregated in a specific area. The law can keep an eye on them to make sure they are clean from disease and to see that girls are not exploited. Also, as they are grouped together, there's less danger that neighbours or innocent women and girls will suffer annoyance.

Not so in Britain where brothels are scattered all over the place, often unhygienic, hard to find, and an annoyance to neighbours. And every now and again the police or a newspaper discover one of these and there is a great blowing of proud and self-righteous trumpets.

One such report describes with relish a 'bargain basement which provides blue films, lewd shows, and the services of women'. It goes on to mention that this particular street is even the home of titled people. And yet, till this report stirred up the dust, I gather that there were no complaints from neighbours. Clients went quickly and unobtrusively in and out and a valuable social service was thus available for inmates of the street and those coming from farther afield. This newspaper report forced it to close.

The law evidently finds it hard to think straight about something so sexually explosive as a brothel. They even have been known to discover brothels 'by mag.c' where others might say that no brothel had ever existed.

Two girls in a flat used to make love to their boy-friends there three times a week. One week one of the girls was out of work and couldn't pay the rent, so she asked her boy-friend if she could borrow the money from him. He made a cheque out to the landlord for the two weeks' rent, and the landlord, much to his amazement, found himself some time later summonsed for living off immoral earnings and running a bawdy house. But was this just? Most people, so I submit, would say that this could hardly be further from a brothel.

The nurses in a hospital were terrified, for, in the night, through the wards and corridors there passed an elusive stranger. Locked doors were opened and a shadowy figure was seen.

Then at 4.30 a.m. one morning, a nurse found a note left in a lavatory. It went as follows:

To the Female Nursing Staff
Dear Nurses,

Please don't be alarmed when you receive this letter. The writer who is very lonely wishes to introduce himself to you.

If any of you will be kind enough to acknowledge his request, you will then realise what love really is from a single man with years of passionate loving saved for the lucky woman.

So come on girls, don't be shy, have heart, from an unbelievably loving admirer of all female nursing personnel.

Your passionate friend.

But it wasn't a timid young nurse who telephoned the number the prowler gave in his letter, it was a woman police sergeant. The number she dialled was a public telephone box, and the man who answered her call admitted he had written the letter. Two policemen who were watching the call box then intervened.

Later, in court, the 'unbelievably loving admirer' was charged with using insulting behaviour likely to cause a breach of the peace. He admitted the charge, saying that his invitation was genuine. 'I've no friends and no female will look at me. I would genuinely like to meet a nurse to go out with her.'

A probation officer also spoke in court and said that the man seemed unable to appreciate he had committed an offence. The man was jailed for three months.

But was this the best way of dealing with him? He had a record of sexual offences behind him, but was this the best use of the taxpayer's money? Would not a kindly and father-like reprimand have been better? Or a date with a nurse?

Another example of the clumsy hand of the law, so I feel, was the case of the man who was warned to keep away from his child's mother.

Fred was blind, aged thirty-five. He had one child by a girl he had lived with, who had become a prostitute. He became worried about the boy when the girl told him that there was no one to look after his child while she was out at work. And so Fred began to spend a great deal of time at her home so that he could be with his son. She helped him out with money, and it seemed a good arrangement.

However, the police stepped in. A chief inspector warned Fred that he would be reported if he continued to associate with the woman. Despite this warning Fred, most understandably, continued to visit the address because he wanted to look after his son who was left alone during the day. He remained inside the premises during the day, looking after his child.

Fred pleaded with the magistrate that he be allowed to continue to see his son, and the magistrate replied with these enigmatic words, 'The circumstances are somewhat unusual in this case and the course I am taking may seem somewhat illogical. It isn't going to be easy for you because although you want to keep in touch with your son, you must keep well away from this woman.'

What a ridiculous situation this seems to be. Why on earth was it necessary to bring this case to court?

The blind man may well have left court with a feeling of outrage that he was being prevented from seeing his son.

Another example of the intrusion by the law into what might seem to the outsider to be perfectly innocent pleasure; the proprietor of a hairdressing and massage organisation decided to add another service for his customers as well, a little sexual stimulation.

The massage was done by a group of attractive girls and he slowly built up a new category of clients, known as 'specials', who, in addition to being massaged, would be sexually stimulated.

Many people would feel that this was a very sensible plan, and indeed, in many countries of the world, such establishments exist providing a more gentle form of pleasure than does, say, a brothel.

However, the police got to know of this and the outcome was severe.

The proprietor had his name dragged through various newspapers when he was taken to court on the grounds that he was running a disorderly house.

Public humiliation and a sharp drop in his male clientele was only a part of the sorrow caused by this act by the police. In addition, one can imagine the worry caused to the wives of men who went to this establishment for massage treatment, and the harm it may have done to many marriages.

Surely in this case it would have been better to let it alone, or at worst, give him a warning? I can think of no possible reason for breaking up this simple pleasure, remunerative to manager and staff, and pleasant for the customers.

Is it good that men should often go away from the law courts with a deep sense of humiliation in their hearts, and hence, in the case of the less sophisticated, bent on revenge? Is this good?

In this, the second part of 'Down and out in Britain', I have been looking at psychiatric hospitals, prisons, and the lawcourts. I have been asking whether they perform well those functions for which they were designed.

The reader must make up his own mind but it seems to me that, to a certain extent, we must accept that, like so much else in the welfare state, they are still in a condition of malfunction.

PART THREE

Homes for the Homeless

The life lived in the institutions which form the typical 'Home for the Homeless' is not considered by most people as typical of the Down and Out situation. But I feel it belongs in this book.

Not only are those whose families have been broken up as a result of Homelessness far more at risk than the rest of the population, far more likely to sink.

But also the insecure children that are bred from these, harrowing experiences of Homelessness are far more vulnerable.

And, what happens to our Homeless is one of the best examples I can recall of the malfunctioning and indeed violence of the welfare state.

People sometimes say, when speaking of my play, *Cathy Come Home*, that Cathy was too attractive, and that so many things could not have happened to one girl.

After visiting a large number of Homes for the Homeless, I can say how amazed I am at the attractiveness of many of the girls one finds there. I sometimes get the impression that such girls are more attractive, not less, than the average girl.

Possibly there is some slight connection between attractiveness and fecklessness – not fecklessness of a major degree, but that little degree of being less scheming than one's neighbour, that can land a girl in Part III Accommodation.

And I think that most people who have had experience of Britain's Cathys will agree with me that the inmates of Part III Accommodation often have life stories more complicated than Cathy's. Cathy basically had less than ten moves. The real life Cathys often have fifty or sixty.

Sir,
 I watched *Cathy Come Home* with great interest, although I broke my heart. My husband and I were in the same position a few years ago.

We know what we should or should not have done, we know our mistakes without anyone rubbing it in. We were both very young when we got married, he was nineteen and in the army and I was only eighteen. I had no parents, but my in-laws warned us what we were up against. Needless to say we would not listen. We first lived in a bedsitter, £3 10s. per week. My husband was in the Forces so I lived alone except for when he came home on leave. Nearly two years later when he was de-mobbed we moved into rooms, we were quite happy, the rent £3 10s. My husband was not getting a big wage but with help from his parents we managed. I was then blessed with a beauti-ful little girl. I was twenty. We could not save as it took all my husband's wages, but we managed quite well always hoping that when my little girl was older I would be able to return to work and save a deposit for a house, but this was not to be, as when my little girl was five and a half years I found I was having another child.

Our troubles were just beginning. We had to vacate our rooms and after endless looking we finally took a house with a very high rent plus rates around six guineas which is all very well on paper but, oh dear, what a terrible struggle it was. I had my second child, a little boy. We lived in this house for twelve months then my husband was off work for nine weeks with jaundice. We got in a mess deeper and deeper. We could pay the rent missing one thing to pay another.

Only those who have been through it know how heart-breaking it is. Anyway we were finally evicted and at the mercy of the council. I was put in a hostel and to cap it all I found that I was pregnant again and I was told by one of those kind council officials who visit the hostels that to become pregnant when you are homeless is worse than being an unmarried mother.

The hostels I was in were much worse than those shown in *Cathy Come Home*. I could write a book on my experience of hostels in the twelve weeks I was in them although it upsets me every time I think about it. It was just like a prison for the women and that is putting it mildly. It was torture for the child-ren who were old enough to understand how degraded their mothers were and how they were treated by the warden.

When I was in there every woman with children under eight had them in hospital with either measles or dysentery. Both my children were in hospital. My little girl had measles followed by bronchial pneumonia and my little boy, then only eight months old, had measles followed by gastric enteritis and I nearly lost him. Both these children were very healthy before going into hostel.

Through all this the husband has to be an outsider looking in, not really knowing what you are going through, watching your children suffer for your mistakes. This causes a lot of ill-feeling between man and wife. I have known it to break marriages up. After twelve weeks in the hostel I was given a sub-standard house for which we were so grateful that the heartache was forgiven but never forgotten. Believe me we suffered for our mistakes.

I implore the councils, close these terrible hostels. Surely there is another way to help young couples who really need help in this generation.

(Letter in a newspaper.)

This is the reality of the life of the Homeless.

Young mothers, who in almost any other country in the world, would have been able to bring up their children and live with their families, are here in Britain often deprived of them.

Thousands of children each year are separated from their parents for no other reason than that their parents can find no home to put them in. Others live with their families in institutions.

Certainly my play *Cathy** was about Britain's intolerable housing lists. But it was about other things too, more important things. It was about compassion and it was about that curious scheme of values which results in local authorities turning people out of 'inadequate' accommodation which in other countries would have at any rate kept them together.

Cathy is a price we pay for clinging to bourgeois ideals of housing. Obviously the answer is to have enough housing for everyone. But, until we have achieved this, I feel that it is immoral to make it so hard for people to live in housing dubbed by the State as inadequate.

D. H. Lawrence speaks somewhere of the dignity of a man building his own house for himself and his dependants. In many countries in the world the majority of houses are still owner-built. Not so in Britain where a succession of regulations make it almost impossible for a man to do what his ancestors did.

Other forms of adequate but 'sub-standard' housing are caravans and boats. Here again there are an intolerable number of regulations which gravely hamper the lot of those who would like to live in them.

It is a question of values. The story is told of a Gypsy passing a Children's Home in his caravan, who enquired what the large building was that he was passing. When he was told, he wanted to go in and take some of these children away with him, to live beneath the stars.

Conversation with a homeless mother in Part III Accommodation:

'Where do you sleep?'

'In the dormitory.'

'How many of you?'

'There's nine women and thirty-nine children. Separate walls each side of you, just a wall each side, you can see straight across to the other beds the other side of the dormitory. The children are running around all the time, especially when the older children are there, you know, and they're running in and out and shouting, you know, I can't get the children, the smaller children to sleep. There are two bathrooms between us and five toilets which you have to share, and there's one copper boiler for each of us to use.

'My eldest, she was never away from her father, when he was around she never wanted me. Being here has upset her quite a lot because every time he says he has to go, she has a cry.

'There was a time when we had to put our children into care.

'Well, when we went to visit them, the eldest one, she's four, just screamed and went away. It broke her terrible, she just didn't want anything to do with us, just went away. Now she's with us in the hostel she has nightmares. And any strange men that come near she just screams, she thinks they're going to take her away. Or if a car comes, you know, I might know someone in the car and go towards it, she'll just run and scream. She's never had screaming fits until we went away. She just wakes up screaming, you know. Sometimes she talks in her sleep, you know, and she says, Get away, get away, you know, as if someone's fighting with her and all that, she just screams.'*

Sir,

Frequently I can see, among the families with which we have to deal here, similar situations arising, and it is necessary to contact various branches of the social services to prevent this.

However, I grow weary of endless telephoning, to be told at every turn, 'This is not our area, our type of case, or our province.'

No wonder there are so many Cathys in this city. To those

who condemn out of hand, and take a 'let them get on with it' attitude, I would say this, 'Without your own good upbringing, with a limited mental ability, an uncooperative marriage partner, too many children and a very sub-standard house, there but for the grace of God, go you.'

(Letter from a Headmistress.)

Sir,

I have met and tried to help a large number of Cathys in the past twenty-two years and never ceased to marvel that large sums of public money are squandered on indiscriminate welfare and so little actually goes where it is most needed.

(Letter from a doctor.)

'I heard a most fearful sound. I took it for the screaming of an animal but it came from a woman. The scene was a derelict remand home in which the LCC temporarily parked homeless mothers and children, but not their fathers. The woman was lying face downwards on a bed and beating her fists into the pillow. Her children, one of them a baby, had just been taken away from her and scattered in various institutions. And she was to be turned out that night, for the excellent administrative reason that the family's time-ration had run out. This practice was soon afterwards relinquished by the LCC but not by dozens of lesser authorities.

'In Kent it has caused the victims to defend themselves with fire extinguishers, but this is exceptional, "We usually find they go quietly," a welfare officer smugly told me the other day. "We get them to see our difficulties." '

(Audrey Harvey in the *New Statesman*.)*

Sir,

The Matron and 'Master' literally tore my sons away from me sobbing, violently, just as you showed in the film, too, while I was in labour with my fourth child and waiting for the ambulance. I could still hear their sobs (they were only seven and eleven years old) as I gave birth to another son just two hours later. I had my second son brought back to me five weeks later, but the eleven year old was put into a boarding school and I only saw him briefly after that during holidays. He, and my daughter, spent most of their time in a Home where they hated it intensely. I very rarely saw my daughter. Once you're down,

107

the Welfare administer the final kick by parting you from your children as quickly as they can.

I had all you showed, cockroaches as well. We had only *one* bedroom between anything up to twenty people (and *one* living room), and used to chase the things with puffer-packs of DDT left with us especially for that purpose. There was a girl there very like Cathy and she was my special friend. Imagine the two of us chasing cockroaches at two in the morning, and actually *laughing* about it!

There are no words to describe the heartache of having your children taken away from you. Specially as you have already lost your home and perhaps your husband. How can the Welfare be so damnably heartless. The pain is physical as well as mental.

(Letter from an inhabitant of a Home for the Homeless.)

'A few weeks ago, a Birmingham-born married couple with several young children were evicted from a service tenancy. They refused to be parted, and so rejected hostel accommodation, a happening not uncommon in Birmingham.

'In desperation they erected a small tent alongside a busy main road in which they then spent several days of misery and despair.

'A child-care officer writes, "Many of my friends have asked, 'Is Cathy really true?' And I have to answer, 'Yes, it is.' " '

(A Birmingham Councillor.)

'Most social workers, even now, see no reason why a family should not be split up, especially as concerns the father.

'Homeless families can become like pathetic yo-yos in inter-borough contests.

'It's like the days of the Poor Law. Different boroughs apply different rules as to the length of residence which will entitle you to their emergency accommodation, some say four weeks, some, six months.

'So anxious are local authorities to avoid the possibility of becoming responsible for a new homeless family that they pack families off somewhere else, sometimes even without letting them stay the night.

'I recall one especially pathetic family who came here from Flintshire because the husband had fallen out of work, and they'd had a violent quarrel with the in-laws with whom they'd been staying. The children were sick, dead tired, weeping and hungry. They were sent straight back to Flintshire.

'Other provincial authorities actually encourage the homeless to go up to the big towns, saying, "We've got no accommodation for you, but they'll give you some there."

'One family like this arrived from the North. We rang their county council and explained that the family were their responsibility. They replied, "We don't want them and we're not going to have them." We threatened to take this up with the Minister and they said, "Well, we agree to have them, but it would not be humanitarian to send them down tonight." We said, "All right, we'll keep them here tonight, and then send them back." We did this. Next morning the pathetic family travelled back up North. They were put through savage and sadistic questioning and that evening saw them back once more in our reception centre.'

(A Local Authority Social Worker.)

'The damage done to the fabric of a family caused by such treatment may well be inconceivable. Children in care as a result of homelessness can be recognised by us because of their very great instability. They are children who have had many moves of schools and homes in a few years. They are not suitable for fostering out owing to their instability. Later they will develop school phobia. It is difficult to see how they will ever turn into normal and happy adults after this treatment in their formative years.

'The National Assistance Act charges local authorities with providing accommodation for families who are homeless in circumstances that "could not have been foreseen".

'Different boroughs interpet this Act in different ways.

'Take the case of a large family on a low income who through poverty and bad management are not able to keep up with their rent. Some boroughs will accept them, others won't. They say that these circumstances "could have been foreseen".'

(A Worker in a Borough Children's Department.)

'I was in rented rooms in a nice house and the owner said, "I'm going to clear the house by March." I said, "You can't do that, it's illegal now." He said, "I can. You'll see." So then he refused to accept my rent for twelve weeks and at the end of this time he took me to court for non-payment of rent. The court found the case proved and said I must be out within a month. At the end of the time the bailiffs came. It was snowing when they came, so they said, we won't turn you out now but we'll be back when the snow goes. They came back and here we are.

109

'An old lady who lived on the floor above me had her rent paid by the social security. When the landlord refused to accept it the social security man came along and said, "If he's not accepting it we're not paying it." After the case she went to an Old People's Home.'

(Inmate of a Home for the Homeless.)

Sir,

Having myself been one of the unhappy throng of homeless, I know only too well the circumstances that prevail in these institutions.

The fact that the families concerned have been through the terrible ordeal of seeing their homes and security snatched from them counts for nothing. They must face this new hazard as though they were, indeed, some kind of malefactor.

Like the untried prisoner, the homeless mother gets a small room furnished with a spring bed and suitable bedding for herself, and one for her children. If there is a baby, a rickety cot is provided. A battered chest of drawers and a wardrobe complete the final touches. Private furniture and utensils are forbidden, and even suitcases under the bed are frowned upon. If she is lucky she gets this to herself, but usually she has to share with another family.

Although married and desperately in need of her husband for support, husbands are also forbidden after 9.30 p.m. To ensure that this rule is rigorously applied, a male porter does a tour of inspection at this time every evening. Human dignity is nil.

There are three meals provided each day, but the quality of these and the conditions under which they must be partaken, are such that those who can possibly afford it, buy their meals out in the local cafes.

The sanitary arrangements are despicable. Dysentery rife, along with many other infectious diseases, but nothing is done to prevent it, nor are the sufferers quarantined until they become so ill that they are rushed to hospital. It is, therefore, almost impossible for anyone to avoid catching something, and the state of the children is pitiful. No sooner are they back from the hospital than they contract something else.

Radios and gramophones are taboo, but there is a broken television set in the dining-hall.

In one place we were in the sleeping quarters were dormitories, each holding the approximate total of eight women and twenty-four children, ranging in ages from eighteen months to fifteen years, and of both sexes. Between them they share three wash-basins and one lavatory minus locks. It is impossible at either of these places to take a bath, there being nothing but a torn piece of curtaining to shield the bather's modesty.

For this I paid, as the mother of three young children, the sum of £5 per week. The charges vary with the size and age of the family.

(Inmate of a Home for the Homeless.)

Sir,

Our eight months of misery began in August last year when my wife and children were directed to a hostel.

While we were there, it was common practice for staff to search personal property without the permission of the families concerned. When I complained, I was told they were looking for cutlery and crockery.

The food at the Big House, as it is called, was fit for the pig trough, after all pigs don't want to identify what is put in front of them before they devour.

It was infected with disease, so much so that I then thought it would be cheaper to transfer the hostel into a hospital than to have the near-constant shunting from there to various hospitals. Infections among children must be expected, but dysentery can only be caused by the lack of proper hygiene and this is the authorities' responsibility.

The staff are very dictatorial, and treated everyone as though they were of low I.Q.

After an argument with a nurse, although she is referred to by a medical rank, she is in fact an attendant, they refused to allow me to see my wife and three children, until the heartless matron decided otherwise. I was escorted off the premises by the police.

Now we live in furnished rooms, happily because we live like human beings and are treated as such.

We now exist as God intended as a family and not as a yo-yo in a transit camp for refugees.

(ex-inmate of a Home for the Homeless.)

Conditions *have* got better in some Homes for the Homeless, probably in most. But in others they seem to have got worse.

A newspaper reported that ten homeless families are turned away each week from the Welfare Department of Brent Council, while council flats overlooking the town hall stand empty.

Investigators in one Home for the Homeless found twenty-seven people of both sexes sleeping and living in one large room.*

'We went into it blind like, you know, getting married, we wanted to get married and we thought it would be easy enough for us to get a flat. We looked round for a flat after we got married and we couldn't find one. All we could find was a caravan which we took, and the first nipper come along and by the summer they wanted us to get out because they wanted it for summer let, and that's how it was going on for about two years, near enough, and then we got this place offered to us that we could live in together and we found it was condemned and the council couldn't do nothing about it, so then they offered us a place in one of their hostels in Colchester. We was there a year, and we wrote to the council after a year, asking if we was, you know, ready for a council house and they said it's like winning the football to get a council house and we thought, well the best thing we can do is put the children away for a little while, while we earn about ninety-six pounds, ninety-two pounds, something like that, to pay down payment on a flat. And we come back to Clacton and we tried finding a caravan, you know, what was suitable for us and the children. We went to an actual caravan site and the proprietor phoned all the caravan sites round the area and they said the least they can sell a caravan for was one hundred and twenty-five pounds down and he said even when you get the caravan I don't know where you're going to put it. So then the missus wanted the children back that much that we had to go and get them back and all they could offer was a place in a hostel for the homeless which doesn't allow husbands, so I have to sleep in the van now.'

Another homeless father, 'Well, I was living in so-called army married quarters, in a caravan at Barton Stacey, and everyone had cleared out at the time, they wanted everyone shifted from the caravan site and I was stuck there and I got a job at Baxters in Andover, as a butcher, and I was working there and I was living in the caravan. I had nowhere to go, the army refused to give me any place to live, help us in any way, put me on a council list, nothing. While we was living on this caravan site they cut our sanitation off, baths, water, they left us a little dingy basin, one tap, had to get water out with my mug to fill the bucket up. Well, one day, when I was at work, the youngest child brought up his stomach contents and he choked to death.

'We left there, because we could stand it no longer, we went to my mother-in-law's, at Peckham. We was overcrowded there, the council told us to get out of there.

'Then we went to my mother's, we stayed there a little while, but my wife and my parents could not get on together, so we left there. We went to my sister-in-law's. The same thing happened there. Then we was out on the street.

'We went to the Welfare. They refused to do anything for us and told us to go back out in the street. I went across the road to the Police Station at four-thirty in the afternoon, I had a few pounds in my pocket and they told me to go back in the street and look for a place. This was four-thirty in the afternoon with three children.

'I went to a friend and asked if he knew any place where I could stay and he is a really good friend, he said, "Well you can stay here," but the landlady didn't want us to stay there because it was a furnished apartment like.

'We stayed there for a couple of weeks and in those couple of weeks I spent pounds looking for a place, it was the same old thing, no children, can't help, no children.

'I tried the Welfare again, they refused because we had slept in the next borough two nights. They told me to go to another Welfare. I went there and that Welfare also refused me; they didn't want nothing to do with us.

'So I just kept on looking and looking and in the end my friend's landlady told me to get out. I had no rent book so I couldn't stay, I had no case.

'So I went back to the first Welfare and I refused to move from the Welfare place itself and so in the end they got me a place in Morning Lane Reception Centre . . . I had made it to a Home for the Homeless.'

Will there ever be found a solution to the inadequacies of Britain's housing? Six years ago the uproar concerning Britain's homeless families caused me to believe that there would be change.

Yet, in despite of all that public uproar, in despite of the fact that a social injustice of which the general public had previously been ignorant was now identified; in despite of the pledges of all parties to solve the housing crisis, and a specific Labour pledge to build 500,000 houses a year, what actually happened?

As Des Wilson has written, in a moving passage; 'My guess is that for all the hullabaloo, Cathy is still homeless. Because, for all the hullabaloo, the emergency end of Britain's housing problem is worse. In 1966, for instance, there were 12,411 people in hostels for the homeless. In 1969 there were 18,849.' (The present total is over 20,000.)

'Greater numbers of casualties can be blamed on greater scarcity – in 1966 there were, for instance, 150,000 families on local authority waiting lists in London. In 1969 these were 190,000.' (The present total is over 250,000.)

'It's possible that Cathy never saw her husband Reg and her three children Sean, Steve, and Mylene again. It's possible that the children are among the 7,000 odd, who will tonight toss and turn in the beds of our children's homes – what we call "in care" – for one reason only – their family haven't a decent home. The bewildered children of beaten parents.

'Most probably Cathy and Reg and the children did come back together again, but now struggle to survive as a family in an over-crowded and squalid slum. Homeless by any civilised definition. . . . Cathy, still in her twenties, will already look old. She'll be apathetic and lethargic. Her skin will be unhealthy, and her nerves will be raw. . . .

'As a nation, we are nearly always foot of the Western European League tables for expenditure on housing. We've never given housing the priority it deserves, and Cathy made no difference to that. As individuals, we never wanted to hear the cries for help before Cathy, and even now we prefer to hear the strident voice of prejudice against the homeless, than to accept the sacrifices we must make to save them.'*

'Desperate families begging for accommodation are being turned away. . . . It is just a matter of how long before the crisis breaks. Families in need flock in crowds for help, but we have just had to shut the flood gates, and close many of our waiting lists. The most depressing thing is that we spend most of our time saying to people: "No chance".'

The spokesman of the London Housing Associations Committee continued, 'It is crisis at the Shelter Housing Aid Centre, where they have reluctantly given up hope of helping even some families in immediate need. It is crisis at the Family Housing Association, the largest of the associations which sprung up in London in the 1960's. Their waiting list has been closed with 800 families already in the queue for the ten new units of accommodation produced by FHA each week.'

And so the tale continues, 'It is crisis in Notting Hill, where the

114

Local Housing Trust closed its list to large families – the ones in real need – two years ago. "Every week ten or twelve desperate families come begging for accommodation and we are in the awful position of having to turn them away," said the Manager of the Notting Hill Trust. "I have the feeling that things are getting worse and worse with the continual reduction in rented accommodation. We have had to close our lists to the larger families who are the ones with the greatest need. The department of the Environment does not seem to be able to recognise the problem." About 250,000 are on waiting lists throughout London for council accommodation. The Boroughs and the GLC are building about 23,000 units a year and vacancies in the 600,000 stock of publicly owned dwellings in greater London occur at the maximum at the rate of 10 per cent each year.'

So, at this rate, it will take thirty years to rehouse even those on existing housing lists, and that only by ignoring the victims of slum clearance.

The crisis can nowhere be better seen than in recent activities of one London council where, 'Families were being evicted on overcrowding orders by the Council itself, and then the Council found itself unable to arrange alternative accommodation.'

Faced with this crisis, one Local Authority went to the unusual lengths of dumping a homeless family and their two children on the doorstep of a house occupied by squatters in an adjoining borough. The husband, who suffers from a recurring blood disease, has been off work for two months because of his illness. A welfare official had told them that no temporary accommodation was available and offered to split the family up by taking the children into care. When they refused to be parted from their children, the parents were told: 'We do have somewhere where you can go.' They were taken to a house already inhabited by squatters and left there.

Another example is that of a Newport mother who arrived home with her two young daughters to find that they had been evicted while her husband was in hospital. The furniture had been carried out of their council house and thrown on to a rubbish tip. An NSPCC inspector protested 'They are destitute. The only possessions they have are the clothes they are wearing. It is disgraceful. Bureaucracy gone mad. The Council spared no thought for these children. This family was £35 behind with the rent. The husband, Fred, who was an unemployed steel worker had had a nervous breakdown a few days before the eviction.'

The wife said that some of the furniture the workmen threw

115

out, including a lounge suite, dining set, two single beds, and a television, was only a year old and still being paid for on HP.

The Housing Manager commented; 'We had to dump it because of its condition.' He claimed that the family was a problem family, and said that they had been warned of the eviction date and should have stored their furniture. Eviction and destruction of their furniture is perhaps one of the more remarkable ways so far devised for helping problem families.

Tom McMillan, M.P. for Glasgow Central, described how a wall and chimney of a tenement building in his constituency had crashed through the houses of 44–50 Fisher Street. 'Last Sunday I visited the house almost next door to the collapse in Fisher Street. The movement in the building was such that the amount of wood cut from the bottom of doors to make them close left a two inch gap. In fact someone who visited the property told me that it was like walking a listing ship. From top to bottom of the building a huge crack has appeared which my constituents point out to me every time I visit the building. They have observed that it is getting bigger.'

The following dialogue between a member of Shelter and a Senior Welfare Officer concerning a family living in a car is quite amazing.

WELFARE OFFICER: We can't help this family. They are not homeless. . . .

CINDY BARLOW: You know they are living in a car, and yet you won't call them homeless?

WELFARE OFFICER: Well, they're not officially homeless.

CINDY BARLOW: Don't you think your policy is unnecessarily rigid if it can't meet a case like this?

WELFARE OFFICER: My authority is official government policy.

CINDY BARLOW: It can't be.

WELFARE OFFICER: My authority is the 1948 National Assistance Act.

CINDY BARLOW: Your authority is not the 1948 National Assistance Act.

WELFARE OFFICER: I think I had better read the Act to you, as you clearly don't know what you are talking about.

CIDNY BARLOW: Don't bother reading the Act, I know what it says.

WELFARE OFFICER: I'll read you the relevant sections as you

don't know what you are talking about. It says the local authority must provide 'Temporary Accommodation for persons who are in urgent need thereof, being need arising in certain circumstances which could not reasonably have been foreseen.'

CINDY BARLOW: And if you read to the end of the paragraph it says ' . . . or in such other circumstances as the authority may in any particular case determine'. Am I correct?

WELFARE OFFICER: Er . . . Yes.

CINDY BARLOW: And you agree that you do have a discretionary power which you are not prepared to use in respect to this particular family which you know is living in a car.

WELFARE OFFICER: Yes.

CINDY BARLOW: Why not?

WELFARE OFFICER: Because they are not officially homeless.

We are told there is a crisis yet see no crisis action. No national housing emergency has been declared. In the last war it was amazing how the pattern of things changed overnight. Prefabs appeared in public parks, where now we build car parks or motor ways. Underground stations were opened for those sheltering from the bombs – but are never opened now for those who sleep out.

Factories switched almost overnight from making cars to making armaments. But they cannot now switch to making houses, although sectional methods of housebuilding now exist, and the parts could be stamped out in car factories.

There are vast gardens, often unkempt, attached to many London houses. But no one has asked their owners to donate them for building for the homeless. Nobody has even seriously thought of going round the under-occupied houses of our big cities suggesting ways to their occupants how they could give some space to the homeless (and boost their own income). We are told that there is a crisis but more and more impetus seems to come from voluntary groups such as the many I have described in this book rather than from the State. Sensible schemes have been suggested such as, in areas of need, taxing rooms above a certain minimum per person which are kept empty. This, too, is not done.

PART FOUR

Children in Care

The reasons for children being taken into care of the State make sickening reading. 'Family homeless due to eviction' – 1,353 children in a year. 'Family homeless for other reasons' – 1,340. 'Unsatisfactory home conditions' – 3,074. All of the first two categories and much of the third are to do with the non-availability of housing. The parents are nearly always blameless.

But housing also sinisterly stands behind other reasons. For instance, who can tell how much the lack of housing is to blame for the tragic stories concealed in 'Child illegitimate, mother unable to provide' – 2,709 in a year. Or 'Abandoned or lost' – 728. Or even 'Other reasons' – the stark figure of 5,381. There are those who say that as many as 20,000 children go into care each year as a result of the State's inability to see that their parents have adequate housing.

And statistics have recently shown that children who have been reared in institutions are more likely to become social problems later in life than are those who are reared outside them.

For all sorts of reasons it is important to ask what sort of life is lived by children in the care of the state.

The official of a charity, whose job is to look after children, tells me, 'Thousands of children like Cathy's each year are taken from their parents, not because the parents are bad parents, but because there are no homes for them.

'In the institutions where they are sent for "care and protection" violence is often done them (although, of course, *most* Children's Homes are run by good and humane people).

'Parents and housefathers in Children's Homes so often demand love from the children. In one Children's Home things had got really wild. There had been a housemother and father that the children loved very much. After that successive houseparents had come there and slowly the children's confidence had been lost.

'Finally a housefather and mother came who were very demanding of the children. They said, "We want you to love us and show your love for us." The children, understandably, couldn't take this. There were wild emotional scenes with the housefather and mother in tears shouting imprecations.

'The children became completely lawless.

'They were separated and the child that was the worst of the lot was sent off to a different Home. And for a while in that Home there was anarchy.

'Children taken into care can feel very lost. Sometimes the fact of being separated from their parents is a traumatic experience that they never get over.

'One little girl used always to be slamming doors. In this State subsidised Children's Home she was always slamming doors, she did it, I think, because no one there was relating to her and she wanted to give herself proof that she actually existed. She needed to slam doors and hear the echo. There was no person there able to give her any sense of her own identity.

'This was after she had been taken into care when her mother died and her father became ill, at the age of nine.

'The superintendent of this Home spoke mockingly to her of this habit.

'When this girl grew up she was unable to give her children the love that she had never received.

'She would reproach her children bitterly for not showing love towards her, but was completely unable to show it to them herself.

'Even years later, after they had been taken into care, she would invite them back to her home, even though by now one of her children had become totally schizophrenic. This child used to rave all the first Saturday of the weekend that he spent with his mother.

'Only now, after years, has she slowly come to realise that it may be her who is mad, not they. And so she has begun to go to therapy classes in order to learn how she can be kinder to her poor children.

'Those who have been hurt may try to hurt others. This is true even when they have no desire on a conscious level to hurt. This woman wants to love her children and have a lovely relationship with them. But she is empty inside and so she hurts them.

'The people who batter their babies are those who are empty inside. When a baby cries it wants love but they have no love to give. Instead they are just reminded by the baby's crying of all the unhappiness which they've had themselves in the past, of all their own crying.'

120

Speaking of one way in which children in care are harmed, my informant said, 'So many people are in social work because of inadequacies in themselves. When the Children's Departments were first formed, there was of course no staff to go in them. So Child Care Officers had to be created and all sorts of people applied, all sorts of clerks and others who still had the old workhouse mentality. The Children's Department started on the wrong foot, but things are getting better now.'

A play leader tells me, 'Despite official government policy not to split up families, all too often children are still taken into care, and all too often they go into different homes when they do go into care.

'The State makes a mess of things. The State can't find them a place to live. And so the children are taken from their parents as "being in need of care and protection".

'They go to a reception centre first. They go for a psychiatrist's report, and one child might come back with the recommendation "he needs to be in a small home with a strong man who could act as a father figure to him, as he comes from a background with a somewhat weak father."

'So then the committee considers this, and at length they come up with the only place that is actually available, and that is a large home with an extremely dominant matron, exactly the reverse of what was recommended.

'Sometimes you get the Child Care Officer telephoning late at night trying to find a place, and the child sometimes ends up, on such occasions, in the local Remand Home.

'And I've known cases, as a result of this, where the child has been so disturbed in this place that he's committed some offence which has resulted in his being transferred to an Approved School.'

So many children are separated from their parents unnecessarily. Many homeless families are not even offered a stay in Part III Accommodation, but are split up instantly.

A scene in many large towns: a house that already has a closing order on it, in which a family is squatting, without electric light, with a large hole in the ceiling where the plaster fell on the little boy as he lay in bed. Outside, a backyard with a high pile of filth and a toilet that never flushes.

The parents who live here with their little boy say that they can't find anywhere else to live at a rent that the man can afford from his lorry driver's wage.

The local authority have been threatening this man, that if he finds nowhere, his child will be taken into care.

A child taken into care because his parents are homeless may be so disturbed that he indulges in unruly behaviour, and for this he will be punished by being sent to a Remand Centre. Here he may again misbehave as a result of his insecurity, and so he will pass on to Approved School, and from Approved School he may go on to Borstal.

A fifteen-year-old girl was remanded to Holloway Prison from a juvenile court because there was nowhere else to send her.

The girl's mother was in tears when juvenile court magistrates made the decision, they said 'with great reluctance'.

Two weeks before, the same magistrates had threatened to protest to the Home Office over the lack of Remand Home accommodation for girls. The girl had admitted breaking into a house with another girl aged fifteen and stealing property worth ninety pounds *after they absconded from a Children's Home*.

But who can say whether it was not the experiences they underwent in the Children's Home that disturbed them so much that they stole? Or the shock of being parted from their parents?

On one occasion five boys and four girls aged between eight and thirteen ran away from a Children's Home.

'It was only an escapade,' explained the city's Town Clerk.

It appears that because they had been naughty, two boys had been refused permission to have tea with the other children, and had been put upstairs with four slices of bread and butter and half a pint of milk each.

After some skylarking the two boys escaped from the Home with seven others and were missing for thirty-six hours.

'If there are allegations of a member of staff nagging children I can only say that this probably does occur occasionally,' said the Town Clerk.

The fact of children absconding from Children's Homes should raise grave questions in the minds of those who administer them.

The new Children and Young Persons Act* should have put an end to some of the violent things done to children. But it's important to realise the sheer awfulness of some of the things that have happened to young children in recent years, and to remember how often attitudes remain, even after they have been in theory superseded by legislation.

At Ealing three girls, aged between twelve and thirteen, had to be put in police cells because no Remand Home could be found for them.

The children had admitted stealing sweets and toys from a

shop. They were taken away from their parents because it was thought they were in need of 'care and protection' and put in the care of the Borough of Ealing.

The Ealing magistrates decided to send the sisters to a Remand Home, but when they checked they found that every single Remand Home from Devon to Durham had been tried without success. No places were available. And so they put these children, who had been taken from their parents because it was thought they were in need of care and protection, into a police cell.

And so the chronicle of violence continues.

One boy ran away from a Birmingham Children's Home and lived in derelict houses for a month, as a protest against being separated from his twelve brothers and sisters who were also in the care of the city council. This boy, whose name was Terry, made temporary homes in derelict houses in the city's Balsall Heath area where the children had lived until their widowed mother died.

Whenever police appeared his friends took him away to another disused building.

The boy was accompanied by his fifteen-year-old twin brothers, Billy and Roy. But the brothers were caught and sent back to the Children's Home. They escaped again and rejoined Terry in the maze of back streets and derelict houses.

Terry even gave a Press conference. His playmates arranged a meeting with newspaper reporters. Terry appealed to the council, 'We will only go back if they will find somewhere where we can all stay together.'

The fact of being separated from your brothers and sisters by the State seems a good reason for absconding. Sometimes, though, the reason is less easy to unearth.

Two nine-year-old girls kept running away from a Monmouthshire Home, 'creating a major headache for the Child Care Authorities and police'.

On one occasion they spent a night sleeping in a barn. The following morning they were spotted by an alert bus driver and were taken back to the Children's Home. Within a few hours they had escaped again.

Almost every day, for a matter of weeks, they escaped, and every time police patrols were alerted to look out for them. Usually they were picked up within a few hours.

On one occasion a bus driver sighted them as he prepared for his first run of the day. He said, 'I saw these two little girls, and knowing that two were missing, I kept them talking. They told me that they did not go to school, they were at The Elms. They said they had been sleeping in a barn, and that they had seen the torches of the police looking for them but hadn't been spotted.

'I got them to help me carry bundles of newspapers on to the bus, and then ran into the office to get the clerk to telephone the police. He took them into the office then and the police were there in minutes.

'The same two were seen at the bus station earlier in the week, but they disappeared again before anyone could stop them.'

What violence, what deception was being done to these children. I could not blame them, after this, for mistrusting the world of adults.

Often, the State's idea of how to provide 'care and protection' seems remarkably inappropriate.

For instance, a magistrate in Farnham, Surrey, sent a disturbed ten-year-old boy to an Approved School for five years because he had played truant from school.

Not everyone in authority acquiesced in this. The Divisional Education Officer for the area said, 'The child is disturbed. It looks like a case of rejection of a child by his parents. . . . I can only assume that their decision to commit the boy to an Approved School was an attempt to find somewhere settled. One would have hoped that it would have been a Children's Home.'

The boy was led from court sobbing and screaming.

And another boy, aged twelve, whose home is in Hackney East, was also ordered to be detained in an Approved School because of truancy.

The boy admitted playing truant from school and stealing a bicycle. The truancy, which his father said was the main charge, was over a period of four months.

The father said his son had been frightened by two older boys at his school who demanded money from him. His son several times returned home with bruises. The parents took him to school in the morning, fetched him at dinner-time, and took him back afterwards when they could. None the less, their son continued to play truant.

The father said, 'We should like him released because he's mixing with boys who have committed more criminal offences and he will be getting into bad company for a long period at the Approved School.'

The bad company and violence of many State institutions makes one wonder whether sending children there is not a case of 'out of the frying-pan into the fire'.

A sixteen-year-old girl was sent to an Approved School because of her love for a married man.

The Chairman of the Court described the man with whom the girl was in love as a 'thoroughly undersirable person to be associated with her'. He followed this arrogant statement by saying that sending her there was in her best interests. But can it be that she was wiser than he?

As the girl was led from the court by two policemen, she screamed and shouted, 'Leave me alone. Don't touch me.'

The girl had been taken into local authority care at the age of fourteen after 'sexual offences' against her by the man who now figured in the case, and who was later sentenced to six months' imprisonment for the offences.

After an unsuccessful stay in a Children's Home, the girl was allowed to return to her stepmother under strict supervision but she started seeing the man again, and 'sometimes stayed overnight'. The County Council solicitor said that there was no proof that the couple were having sexual intercourse.

The man, he said, was a bad character 'morally and criminally' and had convictions for unlawful sexual intercourse with this girl and another. He had other convictions for dishonesty and was currently subject to a suspended prison sentence.

The Children's Department, the solicitor said, felt that the girl's association with him was wholly undesirable and would bring her nothing but unhappiness. They allowed her to go back to her stepmother, but when the promise to end the association was broken an Approved School order was sought.

'A great deal of nonsense has been talked about the order on the basis that it was wrong to send a girl to an Approved School when she had not committed an offence.

'But, according to the Home Office, more than 1,100 children in Approved Schools have not been convicted of any crime but have been sent there for their own protection and welfare. In a recent month there were 1,078 girls in Approved Schools and 724 of them were non-offenders.

'The Approved School system was never intended primarily as a place of punishment but as a place of education and training.'

A Child Care officer said that the girl had always denied any sexual relationship with the man since she was first sent to a Local Authority Home. In an Approved School the girl might meet others convicted of criminal offences and they might have an undesirable influence on her.

The girl said that she was still in love with the man and was not prepared to promise not to have any sexual relationship with him in the future. She said, 'I want to marry him when he is free to marry.'

She was trapped by a solicitor into agreeing that 'she was quite unable to resist that association'.

'You believe he is going to make you happy and care for you, don't you?' asked the solicitor.

'Yes.'

'He has never done it for anyone else,' said the solicitor.

Her defence said that hundreds, perhaps thousands of teenage girls fell in love with married men and it would be an exceptional parent who, faced with this, resorted to sending a child to an Approved School. He added his opinion that a social problem like the one facing this girl could not be solved by removing her from normal community life. If she went to an Approved School she would leave there defiant and embittered towards society.

There was a real possibility that she would meet other girls whose influence might be considerably worse than that of this man.

Who knows?

What is despicable, I feel, is the arrogance of these adults arguing about someone who, morally and intellectually, may have been more adult than they. Did she really love him? Did he love her? Does not sending her to an Approved School make a mockery of the 'care and protection' they were supposed to be giving her?

Might it not be that this girl's love could be the salvation of the man?

Here is another example of a young girl being placed in a State institution.

From a newspaper report: 'A pretty fifteen-year-old girl spoke boastfully to the court of the men in her life, of gangs for whom she was a "call girl", and of the places where they met. "Of course I have been with men, I have them over sixteen, twenty-five and upwards."

' "She is absolutely man mad and does not care what age or colour they are," her mother told the court. "We have found an index book in her bedroom with more than one hundred names listed."

'The girl, wearing make-up and with a mature figure, listened unconcernedly as her mother told why she had brought her to court.'

And what a tragic admission of failure it is, so it seems to me,

126

that a mother was prepared to say such things about her daughter in front of a court.

'When the magistrate said she would be sent to a Remand Home for reports her composure gave way to temper.

' "I won't stay there!" she shouted.

'As a policewoman tried to lead her from the room the girl met her with a rain of kicks and blows.

'A Warrant Officer went to the policewoman's assistance and the girl kneed him in the stomach. Together, they got the girl into the Warrant Office where she pulled over furniture and scattered chairs, books and papers over the floor.

'When another Warrant Officer went to their aid the girl grabbed him by the tie and kicked his shins.

' "It really all started four years ago," said the mother. "She was a continual truant from school and though I took her every day in the car and fetched her from the school gates she never went into school but wandered the streets.

' "At home the girl's behaviour was objectionable. She was utterly disobedient and resented being spoken to.

' "The climax came the other week when she took an enormous overdose of phenobarbitone and luminal tablets," the mother went on. "She was rushed to hospital where she was unconscious for three days."

'Referring to her daughter as being "a call girl" for several gangs, her mother said, "Lately I have been returning from work and having to turn men out of the house.

' "It has come to the point where I must watch her every second because of her reactions to men. It is all making me ill."

'The girl told the court she agreed with the complaints made against her, adding, "I don't care what happens. I am the girl for the gangs from Paddington, Kensington, Hammersmith and Putney, and I do not think it is wrong." '

Was locking her up a solution? Or could it be that, in her rejection of the bourgeois standards of the place where she grew up, this girl, albeit violent, was in fact more adult than those who sentenced her?

Some Children's institutions have had their names changed to Community Homes, but it is important to remember that the buildings and the people who run them will remain the same, although there will obviously be an attempt to change some basic attitudes. Others, including Borstals and Detention Centres, won't be renamed.

The violence done to children in various institutions cannot be justified even by a fall in the number of convictions.

Figures quoted by Mary Iles* showed that of all boys discharged from Detention Centres 66.2 per cent of juniors and 58.2 per cent of seniors were reconvicted.

And of those who had first been to Approved School and then sent on to Detention Centre, 87 per cent of the juniors and 79.7 per cent of the seniors were reconvicted.

The National Council for Civil Liberties also commissioned a report* and this concluded that since the regime of Detention Centres was calculated to break the will of offenders in the shortest possible time, committal to a Detention Centre was a 'flagrant denial of every principle of rehabilitation'.

A group of ex-detention boys who were selected by their probation officers as being truthful had this to say about their experiences:

'Some officers are all right, some are strict. They may need to be to maintain discipline, but it made you feel like hitting them back.'

'Two or three are good and like a bit of fun, a joke. The others, you have to call them all sir, they treat you like you're a prisoner, like you're a robot. It makes you hate them.'

'X dragged a lad who had asthma around the field. You had to run round three times wearing heavy boots. This lad was starting to go blue because he couldn't breathe, and he said he couldn't make it. X said, "You'll make it." And he dragged him and kicked him round.'

'If anyone talks after hours in the dormitory, everyone has to stand out of bed for an hour, even if they have been asleep. This happened about a couple of times a week. During the period of my detention it happened about five times in the middle of the night between one and two o'clock.'

'My first night in the dormitory the lads were messing about because I was new. The officer came in and told everyone to get out and stand by his bed; then he hit me in the stomach hard enough to wind me.'

'My mate who was at the Centre because of absconding from an Approved School, was taken to the Detention Cell Block and made to scrub dustbins with sandpaper. The officer on duty would come in the night, wake him up, and say, "Are you all right?" And give him a clout, "Go back to sleep then." '

A father felt that his fifteen-year-old daughter was mature enough to get married. Therefore, as she was legally not allowed to, but was deeply in love, he forged her birth certificate and she was married to a husband aged nineteen. The ruse was discovered.

Immediately after the wedding the girl was snatched off into the care of the State, and put in an institution. The father said, 'She was not going to go back to school after the wedding. They were going to live part of the time with his parents and part of the time with us. He had put down a £50 deposit on a house where they were going to live.' The girl's mother added, 'I have not slept because of the worry. The only thing I have managed to do is to get back my girl's ring which the police took.'

PART FIVE

In an Unmarried Mothers' Hostel

Dear Sir or Madam,

I have been going out with a boy for nearly two years. Now I find I am pregnant, four months I think, but I am not sure how you calculate the time. I don't think he will marry me, if he was going to he would have asked me by now as he knows I am pregnant.

I haven't seen a doctor as he knows my parents very well, could you put me in touch with another doctor, I do not get on with my father and it couldn't possibly work staying at home, that is of course assuming they'd want me.

I am nineteen and a half years old and at present employed as a typist. I've got to see someone soon to find out if I will be able to support my child, I will do anything in my power to do so.

I have enclosed a s.a.e. for your reply,

Yours faithfully,
Jean M.*

Many thousands of girls each year pass through Homes for Unmarried Mothers and it is time that a society calling itself humane had a closer look at what goes on in them.

A study by Jill Nicholson† found that some of the Homes are excellent. But in too many others, at a time when a girl is especially vulnerable, she is sent on a spiritual obstacle course. At a time when she in in need of help and sympathy she is victimised by a series of obsolete, repressive, vindictive rules and regulations.

Jill Nicholson found that sometimes the residents of hostels for unmarried mothers were not allowed out at all on Sundays, except to church. Cards, games, the record-player, and television were forbidden; so were high heels, make-up, slacks and bus rides. Housework was often excessive.

In only a small number of Homes were the mothers quite free to choose whether to breast-feed or bottle-feed their babies. In the others, they might be encouraged, persuaded, or almost forced to adopt the method of feeding favoured by those who were looking after them.

In half the Homes, she found that mothers were free to go and see their babies whenever they wanted to, but in others they actually had to ask permission before going in to see their own babies.

One matron explained that this ruling was necessary because some girls were a nuisance; always running in to pick up and cuddle the babies. She seemed to feel that this was unreasonable.

Often residents were not allowed to take their babies out for a walk in the afternoon.

A girl told me, 'I went to ask the matron whether I could be excused breast-feeding my baby. The thing is, I was going to have him adopted, and I thought, if I breast-feed him, I'll become involved with him to the point that it would be very hard to give him up.

'I put this to the matron, but she told me that the Hostel doctor favoured breast-feeding, and not to breast-feed my baby would be not giving him the best start he could have in life.

'So I did breast-feed him. And I became involved with him. And now I've got to give him him up, and don't know how I can face it.'

Another rule in some Hostels is that babies may not be picked up before the set time for feeding them. The babies are left to cry.

Obviously, in any institution, some rules are necessary. But not this sort of thing.

In one place visited by Jill Nicholson, even the girls' fathers had first to ask permission before visiting. In many Homes, boy-friends were not allowed to visit, however close their relationship might be to the girls who were bearing their babies.

One matron said she didn't want 'a lot of young boys littering round the place'.

This seems especially sad in that, in Homes where boy-friends *had* been allowed to visit, some matrons said that the first sight of the baby so touched them that 'it had been the making of some marriages'.

Over seventy thousand illegitimate babies are born each year, or one out of thirteen of all babies.* Of these, several thousands will spend their first few weeks in one of these hostels.

Some of them are happy. I met one delightful matron, a little old woman whose cheerfulness and compassion made all the girls love her.

Such places are sometimes very pleasant. Sitting in them, talking to the girls and the staff, one's only regret can be that it was necessary for the girls to become pregnant in the first place.

The matron of one such place said to me, 'It's like a peep behind the scenes, when one gets to know about these girls and their stories. The word is "accept". If only our society could accept more what people actually do, and not judge them by what it feels they should do.'

A girl, speaking of Christmas at one such Hostel in the North told me, 'We didn't have a very good family background. This was the first Christmas, the first real Christmas, I've ever known.'

Other Hostels have birthday parties and excursions for the girls.

Such are the nice Hostels. And as we become a more humane society, more and more Hostels are becoming like these. But there are others which seem to be unfortunately bedded down in too much of the old atmosphere of punishment.

Some of the saddest stories concern girls grieving after they had had their babies adopted (because they could see no way of keeping them in this often hostile society). One, weeping, was taunted by a matron, 'There's not much point in crying. You've only got yourself to blame. Why did you give it away?'

Another girl, as a result of an administrative error, had to hang on and hang on to her baby, waiting for it to be adopted, and as the weeks went by and she became more and more attached to the child, other girls at the Hostel said they could see her ageing.

A sinister discovery is that the serve-'em-right attitude of 'back to the penitentiary' is more prevalent not in the old-fashioned North, but in the more 'modernistic' South.

More girls in the South tried to hide the fact of their pregnancy from their family. They had fewer visitors, were more likely to have left their job when they became pregnant, and were less likely to have a job to go back to. They were more anxious to hide from neighbours.

Jill Nicholson says, 'We never heard in the South, as we did in the North, of workmates who had a collection before a pregnant girl left, or of neighbours who knitted for the baby, or sent magazines and chocolates when a girl was in the Home.'

About three per cent of all girls interviewed had been actually turned out of the house by their parents when they became pregnant.

A newspaper report of one Hostel revealed how the girls there

133

were fined for petty breaches of discipline, turned out of bed on occasion for a 'defaulters parade' and ordered to rake through dustbins full of ashes to salvage bits of coke.

It also described how, 'girls go down to the kitchen in the night to heat milk for their babies. Matron is a light sleeper and if she wakes up and sees that someone has left the light on she rouses everyone. All the girls go downstairs and she asks them who left the light on. If someone owns up they are fined half a crown on the spot. Of course, the babies wake up and there is bedlam.' This defaulters parade was also called as a result of other misdemeanours.

A girl who was a at Catholic Hostel told me, 'A priest came once a day to make us ashamed. The day after my baby came we were back scrubbing floors.'

Reports by girls themselves about Hostels they were in may of course be tinged with their own neuroses. But it should be remembered that this neurosis is itself part of the story. Why are the girls neurotic? Do the Hostels contribute to this neurosis?

Girls in this state of pregnancy need more than rational treatment. Often they fear persecution when in fact there has been none, and that is why those who look after them should be so careful. A report I had from one girl claimed, 'The Sarcastic Secretary, we called her: she was a frustrated spinster who loved poking fun at our babies and our swollen bellies. She loved to catch me in the corridor and say, spitting out the words, "Well, what are you going to do when you've had your baby? Then your troubles will really begin." A hundred times each day she would ask me that question, until my head was in a whirl, and I ran to the chapel for peace and quiet.'

At another Home I have had reports of the matron actually stopping the daily service and calling girls up in front of her because, so she said, they were 'rushing the hymns'.

Girls at another Home were constantly terrorised with the threat that they would be forbidden to go out at all that day if they didn't do certain jobs within a certain period.

One of the strangest rules I have heard obtained in another Hostel, where girls were only given a limited time in which to feed their babies. If their babies hadn't finished feeding by then they had to be put back in their cots, regardless of whether they had had enough.

One girl described this by saying, 'They rush you, and it's no good, the one thing you can never do with a baby is rush it.'

A similar, inexplicable rule in one Hostel concerned a lavatory.

The lavatory in the garden was for the girls to use. The lavatory in the Hostel was exclusively for the use of the staff.

Of course, the point must be made that so much of what the girls complain of in Homes for Unmarried Mothers is due to lack of funds for this unpopular cause.

A girl tells me, 'I really enjoyed my stay at the Mother and Baby Home, both at the Home and in hospital. Everyone was extraordinarily friendly and helpful.

'The only thing was the heating, and that was dreadful. My baby came back from the well-heated hospital to the icy nursery at the Home and was so cold that she cried day and night.'

The idea of preventing the girls getting too involved with the babies is sometimes used to justify some of the Hostel rules, such as the one which says that girls may not take their babies out at all, or take their relatives to see them.

'Adoption societies,' so a matron told me, 'who insist that the unmarried mother should care for her baby herself for six weeks, should be made aware of the mental suffering caused by allowing the mother to develop a natural deep affection for her baby, when it has already been decided that the baby is to be adopted. The agony at the handing over of the baby is quite an unnecessary part of this already unhappy situation and is not, in my view, in keeping with Christian principles.

'This has been brought to my notice more forcibly as I have recently been concerned with an eighteen-year-old unmarried mother-to-be who has been faced with this situation. She has strong maternal instincts already and has found the decision to have her baby adopted a most difficult one, though it is the only possible decision in her particular circumstances. Much unnecessary suffering would have been caused by having to care for her baby at home for six weeks and then part with it, a punishment surely no Christian would wish to impose.

'Fortunately it has been arranged that the baby will be cared for by the Local Authority for this period. The girl will pay, most willingly, for this. Why cannot this be normal practice?

'I have been told by the adoptive parents that they have been made aware of the heartbreak of the mother when they went to the Home to collect their child and naturally they too were extremely distressed. If the public was aware of this I am sure that something could be done to put an end to this lack of understanding.'

'I remember going back from the doctor in the bus, thinking,'

"This can't be true. . . ." '

'I mean, I think it will affect all my life really, because no matter where you go, even if you had the child adopted and you see small children you just remember what your own child looked like, you know. . . . '

'I think the best thing of all is to work very hard, keep your mind occupied, that's the best thing. . . . '

'Well, I've got to try to forget him, that's one thing, but it's going to be very hard because I still think of him every night. . . . '

'There should be some punishment. I think that men that do that sort of thing should be punished. . . . '

This is how unmarried mothers talk.

They come from all professions. They can be doctors, nurses, lawyers, debs, clerks, shop assistants, machinists, dressmakers, waitresses, factory girls, girls not yet at work, air hostesses.

Yet from the way they are often treated you might well get the impression that pre-marital love-making was practised in Britain only by a tiny proportion of trollops and fallen women.

'Everyone was doin' it, you know, when we was at school, people said, "What, aint' you done it yet?" You got to feel the odd one out, then you got worrying, what, don't no one want me? Listening to the songs, you know, open your arms, lead me to ecstasy, all that when you're goin' with a fella. Well, of course, it was old muggins here. When I finally had a go, of course I fell for a baby. . . . '

'We weren't going with a lot of fellas, you know what I mean. Just going with the fella we was going with. But if you don't these days most fellas will get hold of a bird what will. . . . '

Some would say that these girls are the inheritors of a new pagan morality, gleaned from the pop song and adman and Hollywood culture. They mature at an age when their mothers did not know where babies came from. They get drunk, make love in the backs of cars, front parlours, deserted classrooms.

Some may feel that they are the product of a culture that holds out sex as an ultimate orgiastic glory, without adding, 'If you don't use contraception you're going to have a baby.'

One quality in a large number of the girls I talked to was their innocence.

'I wasn't a fast, loose girl, some people say it's the bad girls fall for the babies. But we were the ones that were trusting and we didn't dream of "taking precautions" because we loved the man so much that our love-making was spontaneous. . . . '

'He's behaved very badly towards me, seeing I'm pregnant, he'd rather have me get rid of the child rather than go out with me. He's turned very nasty against me, and yet before he was very much in love with me. But once he found out I was pregnant he was changed completely, he was just like another person. . . . '

Quite a high proportion of the girls come from broken homes and may themselves be illegitimate and from Children's Homes.

They are the girls who have never had anything. They have no friends, no security. They are unkempt, of low intelligence, and their boy-friends may be in prison. They are the wash-ups of society, often never having known love and finding the world confusing and cruel.

For them, this double rejection, first by their folk and then by society, can have effects hard to calculate. These are the girls, for instance, who are thrown out of their homes and arrive at one of the big city termini. They are befriended by one of the men who are always hanging about, are passed on, and pass through many hands before they are finally abandoned.

Urban areas have the highest illegitimacy rate. One reason for this is the prevalence of the bedsit girls. These are the girls who leave home and come to the big cities for excitement, or for other reasons.

'My parents were among the better class of person in Chingford. I had a quarrel with them about staying out too late, so they said it was better I went on my own. I got a job and a bedsitter in Kensington. Then came the summer and people went away for their holidays. I got lonely. I started going to parties round Kensington. I drank a little too much at one of them, a boy saw me home, and it happened. He said, "That'll be all right." The next thing I heard, he was in the South of France. . . .'

A lot of these lonely girls come from abroad, particularly Southern Ireland and the West Indies. Girls coming from stable communities often find that they have few weapons to compete in the jungle society which now exists in large areas of our great European cities.

'I was leaving Sligo because it was so tight on me, there were no dances, you couldn't go to the pictures without your mother was there to take you. It was then that my mother died. I was sad. I've always been lonesome, I find it hard to make friends. I came across the water. I got myself a bedsitter. Soon I thought I'd got a friend at last, and I got over my lonesomeness. When I'd known him two years I sinned. He said we were going to get married. We many times sinned. Then I found a letter addressed to him from a

137

woman with his name written on the back. It was from his wife. Being Catholics we could never get married. I left him then. I didn't want to see him again because I think if I do I will hit him. . . . '

Then there are the married men's darlings, secretaries and receptionists who form liaisons with men older than themselves at the office. Such men have a great fascination for some, they are mature, and yet they need to be mothered and understood and they carry with them the romantic aura of an illicit relationship.

There are other married men who deceive their girls and who counter the girl's alarming revelation that she is having a child with the doubly alarming one that they are already married and themselves have many children. Then it is a battle for his affections between girl-friend and wife. The wife (such is habit) usually wins.

Many of the babies are the despair rockets of older single women.

'There are so many young girls coming up all the time, a girl gets to the age when she'd like to marry, and she realises that, without her noticing even, it's become too late. She's too old. There's too many younger girls coming up. So that's how you get almost split in two with wanting to have a child. So when you're with a man, one side of you that is stronger at that moment than any other says, "Yes, I'm going to have a baby, I'm going to, then they'll *have* to let me. . . . " '

Other illegitimate babies are born to a certain hard core of backward, lone women who find it hard to stop having children; the sort that in less liberal times used to be locked in asylums. They are often pleasant to speak to and weak-minded only in this one respect, running up large totals of illegitimate children.

A Welfare worker gave me the following story (but others say that they believe it to be apocryphal), 'I was told that there was an unmarried mother in a remote part of Norfolk, and that I must go to see her. I found her in an antique, decrepit sort of place, absolutely surrounded by children. She was a simple but kindly woman. I asked her if the children were hers. She said they were. I asked her where the father was, and she said, "Well, he lives here with us!" So I said, "Excuse me asking, but why aren't you married?" She said, "So we would be, but twenty years back I was in hospital with a fractured spine. I was there a year. When I was leaving the doctor took me aside and said, 'You'll be all right for everything now except one thing: there's one activity you must never indulge in. . . . So,' said the man, 'I'm telling you, for your own good. You must never marry.' " '

What about the fathers of illegitimate children?

Many unmarried fathers seemed to me irresponsible. They were against men using contraception, alleging that this made the experience of love-making like having a bath with one's boots on. One told me he used contraceptives to allay the fears of his girl-friends, but in fact sabotaged them by drilling holes in them.

An Irish labourer told me, 'I had the two of them four times each that night. Then a few weeks later one of them come and said she was up the creek. I said, "Fair play to yourself, my dear, and I'm back to the ould countrie!" '

And a secretary, 'Men these days want just one thing, the session on the sofa. They expect it in return for taking you out. Often I've had to fight my way out of dinner dates.'

Not all fathers of illegitimate children are like this. They often love their girls and are prevented by circumstances from marrying them. There is a lot of tenderness in innumerable illicit affairs, before the final disaster. But the old Victorian idea of despising a girl if she yields is adhered to by an alarming number.

The privations of the unmarried mother trying to make a go of things with her child in some lonely bedsitter have been described to me by a girl as, 'Those things which are not always apparent on the surface, the doing one's own shoe repairs to save cobbler's bills, living on flour and water in order to give guests a decent meal, borrowing from one meter to fill up another meter, and the very borderline relationships with men that are almost prostitute/client but not quite, even though money is exchanged.

One learns to avoid paying for things. It is not so much poverty, unmarried mothers seem quite good at keeping above poverty line without actual money. They can own a fur coat but have no shoes for their children. The only class that will accept the unmarried mother is the Bohemian class.'

An illegitimate girl told me, 'First I went to Somerset House to get my birth certificate. But as I had been given an incorrect name at the orphanage they told me that no one of that name had ever been born in Britain.

'I went back to the orphanage and ascertained my correct name. With this I was able to get my birth certificate.

'Then I decided to find my mother. I wrote to her, and later arranged to meet her. But my mother stood me up. I made a second arrangement. This time, she said she'd be sure to come. But once more she didn't. After all, it's her life. I suppose it shouldn't upset me.'

Another girl told me, 'I am an illegitimate girl, born of probably working-class parents, shortly after the last war. I was adopted by a middle-class couple, whose families have wholly accepted me. When I was eight or nine I began to want to find my real mother, not to live with her, I love my step-mother too much for that, but to know what she was like, and what kind of life she lived. When I reached the age of sixteen I decided to write to every nursing home and hospital in the area where I was born, to see what they could tell me. However I was unable to get any help.

'Everyone at school is very friendly and never mentions my adoption, but I feel a difference, probably imaginary, accentuated by the fact that I am at a public school.

'I was also worried by the fear that prostitution is an hereditary "disease". It is a horrible thought and has made me too scared to kiss a boy. I am so worried that I would be unable to control my emotions.

'I will also feel bound to tell anyone I know that I am illegitimate. I wonder what their reactions will be, and how many "friends" I will lose.'

Another girl told me, 'Personally I had no idea how bad it could be for some of these illegitimates until I met a crowd of them at a reunion a couple of years ago. The only incidents in my own life have been the well-meant "Ah well, it's not your fault" which one can be neurotic enough to take as an insult, and the priest who told me that "bastards are a curse in the eyes of God". For some of the others, however, the problem is beyond a joke. Most of the boys I grew up with, for example, graduated automatically from the school to the Army. They find that they are unable to get a commission except on a field of battle. This, from an institution which pretty well founded the breed! The C.O. tips them off confidentially, in a fatherly manner, that with their birth certificates, it's best not to press the matter. This is only one instance. There are a lot of cases where it has left a scar. As you know, society at large is pretty tolerant, the individual is another matter.'

Another girl, 'I hope my own child will not be ungrateful for having been brought up by her own mother. My parents were married in the last war because I was on the way, and ever since I knew this, I have often thought how proud I'd have been of my mother if she had brought me up on her own.

'Many articles have been written on the mental adaptation of an adopted child and that of a child brought up by its natural mother. Most of them agree that, while adopted children go to good homes, where they have everything they want, nobody can really take the place of the natural mother. After all, why do so many try to find their true mother? I admire girls who have the courage to part with their babies, although I could not, but let not our children condemn us for it!'

'I was studying medicine and the father was also a medical student. What happened when I became pregnant? Well, I was sent down. He was only suspended and later he was allowed to return to complete his studies.'

'Men can boast of their conquests in love but women have still to keep their secrets. Oh for equality in love and sex, where neither side can deride the other! If society could be educated to accept and realise the problems involved and if they could forgive, there would be far less unhappiness and psychological stress suffered. There is nothing worse, in my opinion, than to be made to feel so degraded and unwanted, a "fallen woman" in fact.

'What strikes me most forcibly is the perverted attitude of society which practically forces the unmarried mother into living through a fundamentally important experience in a totally twisted and unnatural manner.'

Another girl told me, 'Having a baby in whatever circumstances is surely the most natural function a woman performs during her life. The desertion of the father is indeed hard to cope with, but the rejection of a child conceived in love and born with pain is surely the most unnatural of deeds. Giving away the baby means that for many, life will be meaningless for many years to come.'

I remember a girl who had to give up her baby. A girl who was totally altered by saying goodbye to it, turned from a decent happy girl into something that was grey, screaming, no longer in control of herself. Constantly returning to the room where the baby had been, unable to prevent herself looking at the cot, looking at the dirty clothes.

How much longer will the illegitimate bastard be discriminated against?

Love-making is very common these days. We live in a sexy world. Everywhere there is the urge towards love, towards romance, towards sex.

In a society that holds up 'love' as this ultimate virtue, how can we still have the face to discriminate (as we still do) against these children born of 'love' and their so often innocent mothers?

There is so little information available even now about what may happen to those who follow the pressures of society and actually do make love.

There is still all too little sex instruction in schools. Contraception is still far too hard to come by.

The unmarried mothers are so often those who take the sexy pressures of our society at their face value, and are then punished hard.

'The days when the unmarried mother was automatically separated from her child are, of course, long past.' So claims a recent report.

But unmarried mothers *do* still separate from their children so frequently, and the death rate among illegitimate children* is so much higher than among the legitimate, that we may feel that the social effects piled up against the unmarried mother are such that the result is, all too often, that she still *is* automatically separated from her baby.

No girl is the same after having a baby. Whatever their attitude before they've had it, these one out of twelve mothers, from the moment that they actually see their baby are in some way committed. And yet, for those who want to keep their babies, the balance is often very heavily weighted against them. A recent report says, 'It is shocking that in the twentieth century, sometimes described as the age of the child, the unmarried mother has so little real freedom of choice. Often, if her real wish is to keep the child, she cannot carry this out because so few facilities are available . . . there is practically no accommodation in this country for the unmarried mother who wishes to make a home for her child. . . . '

The trudge around town with her baby, looking for lodgings with landladies slamming the door in her face often as though she were unclean, does something to a girl's confidence. She may find a bolthole at last and get her child into a nursery and herself a job. But what if the child falls sick and she has to stay home to nurse it, and her boss ultimately loses his patience? Some girls heroically battle through the bedsit jungle of our big cities, then finally write a sad letter to the adoption societies.

Fifteen thousand illegitimate babies each year are adopted.† But there is another way. In the case of two and a half thousand children taken into local authority care each year, the statistics give the reason, 'Child illegitimate, mother unable to provide'.§

These are the children who go into care because often the mothers think that later they'll be able to take them out again. Such children may go on for year after year, deprived of the real chance of a home because of their mothers' belief that one day, some day, she'll be able to create a life for them.

142

Other problems face the unmarried mother. If she has her child adopted she has three months to think about it before she must sign a final document giving total control of her child to the adoptive parents.

As the time to sign approaches, many mothers become more and more scatty. On receiving the form girls have been known to become highly unbalanced and run away from everything.

'I took to the fields, working on fruit picking and later on potatoes and swedes. I lived in the huts where the workers are put up, but a man who was working with me came after me and raped me, and after this I slept out. It was a very hot summer. Finally, one day, in a highly dishevelled state, I arrived at the baby's adoptive parents' home, and said I must have the baby back.'

The matron of a Hostel told me, 'I've been with girls after rooms, the landladies won't take them. The girls get depressed. They have to pay someone to look after their babies. They feel rejected and the result of this is, they cut themselves off. So often then the girl's health breaks. The baby gets ill, perhaps bronchitis. And then, baby clothes are such a terrific price these days.

'The girls as often as not lose contact with their caseworkers. The caseworker will say, "If you get into trouble come and see me." But that isn't enough. The girls may well be too worried to take the initiative. They need expert treatment. The social worker says, "Come any time", but the girls know how busy they are, and the sort of thing they need help on may not be anything specific but rather that their whole life is in a mess.'

Another girl who fought heroically to keep her baby but finally had to give it up, describes the situation in these words, 'When your baby goes you're sort of numb inside because of what you've lost. I mean you've lost the most important thing you've ever had in your life, and you know nothing about the outside world because you've lost contact with it, you've been in here you've talked nothing but babies and thought nothing but babies for about three months, and then you go out and you don't know what people are talking about, you don't know any of the latest gossip and of the latest jargon.

'I'd like to have kept my little girl, I think so much of her. But my parents said it would ruin my life, and I mustn't take her home.

'And the girls do love their babies, and if they give them up it's not because they don't love them. When mine went I couldn't feel, I couldn't think, it's all right if you keep your mind occupied, but you'll always be remembering when you see another girl with her child, that once you had a little baby, too, and then gave it away.'

Britain's hostels for unmarried mothers are not a popular charity.* People collecting for this cause are all too often informed that they are subsidising sin.

And so they are – the sins of the State, a State that allows a constant incitement to sex but still makes information, contraception, abortion,† all too hard to find; causes thousands unwillingly to have their babies adopted or taken into care; or to have their babies too young to be able to cope with them,§ and in many hostels punishes them.

Now at last flatlets are being opened up for unmarried mothers, but there are all too few of them and they are not always ideal places. A very common regulation concerns boy-friends, for instance. Boy-friends have to be out of the place by 11.30 p.m., but this does, of course, make it hard for a girl to get to know a man whom she might then like to marry.

'It isn't that we object,' say the people who make this rule. 'But it's the neighbours, and above all the police. The thing is that the police threaten to close down this place as a brothel.'

There is no cure for illegitimacy. When it occurs the individuals concerned place themselves outside society. For the mother who keeps her child, not only she, but both herself and child, continue to be subjected to stresses and strains, financial and emotional. Thus a mother wrote to me, 'Yes, society exacts its price. It is to be hoped that she can still salvage from this tragedy some strength to go on living effectually. The mark of this experience will never be removed.

'You see I know, my child has just been adopted.'

PART SIX

Conclusion: the Violence of the State

In the course of writing this book I have visited some of the darker sides of Britain's affluence.

It has struck me how the State, founded in the name of Christianity and love, so often kicks in the teeth those very people who are in need of support and help. Some of the most sensitive people who could be of use to the State, it converts instead into criminals or lunatics,

It is an old saw that armies have a vested interest in wars since that gives them status and identity.

It is an old joke that lawyers, solicitors, social workers, judges, magistrates and policemen have a vested interest in the creation of criminals and other failures, since otherwise they'd be out of a job.

But it may be more than just a joke.

As well as the good they do, there is an immense amount of harm that they do. Often it is amazing to see how alienated these people are from the suffering that they see before them, and to which they contribute, and how remarkably lacking many of them are in any sense of basic humanity or love for their fellow human creatures. People capable of such naivete are also capable of other psychological blunders. They must be helped to learn self knowledge.

They must understand that there is a strong underside in all of us that thirsts for violence.

Magistrates, for instance, should understand why it is that criminals say that they give harsher sentences just before they eat.

After the First World War we crippled Germany, with humiliations so grave that it was, so some have said, almost inevitable that she would return to attack us in order to recreate her self-esteem.

Do we not do that again and again to those whom we send

through the courts, often on trivial charges? And do we not thus create a group of people at war with their own society?

Even if a man is completely sorry for what he's done, the law still feels that he should be punished for it. The law does not believe in the Christian attitude to this. The law believes in absolute evil and absolute retribution.

It has been said that the law courts represent in symbolic form a fight between good and evil, that fight that we believe is going on in all of us individually.

It has been suggested that we allot roles to people in our immediate circle, to one person we allot the role of scapegoat, to another that of villian, to another of clown, to another that of father figure, and so on.

So there is a danger that those who are in charge of the administration of justice may be tempted to allot the role of criminal to someone who is not really a criminal And there is a strong temptation for the police to do the same, since their way of life depends on the existence of crime and thus there must be a strong compulsion (not usually at a conscious level) to create criminals even if the material is not quite appropriate.

If we are honest, we must admit that much of our justice is of a very rough kind, based on vindictiveness, not compassion. So often a man in trouble who desperately needs help is instead kicked through the courts.

Behind the courts stand the police.

At one time people thought of the police force in terms of 'the strong arm of the law', the warm protecting father's arms. What phrase comes into many people's minds now? As the policeman approaches us down the street, as he rides by on his jabbering motor cycle, as he looks at us with that cool contempt which has nothing to do with protectiveness, a more likely phrase to describe him might be 'the surly lip of the law'.

May not the police create an aggressive attitude in us by their own aggression?

My proposal is that the police should be promoted for the positive acts they do, rather than the negative ones.

They should be promoted for those ways in which they have helped society, those ways in which they have *prevented* crime, rather than for those ways in which they have punished, endorsed, or even created it.

But the rot runs in deeper than that. For, although our national standard of living is higher than ever before, there is none the less at the moment still a steady increase in the number of people admitted into prison, Children's Homes and Part III Accommodation. The number of admissions to mental hospital remains constant.

The British institution appears to have achieved almost a life of its own, sucking in always, more and more people.

The institution can be like a vast monster that, however good its physical amenities, maims us mentally, turning out spiritual morons, those who look and speak like real people, but do not act like them.

Frank Foster, the Director of Borstal After-Care, says, 'Some time ago I was talking to a social worker from a newly emergent country. I asked him for his impression of Britain. He said, "What impressed me most was the number of old people and children who were lonely, homeless, or in institutional care. In my country the old are honoured and looked after by their families and the orphan too is taken into the home of his relatives or friends. They are not cast out. . . . So many Old Pople's Homes, so many Children's Homes in Britain, it is sad." '

There are twenty thousand people in Homes for the Homeless, 170,000 admitted annually to psychiatric hospital, and thirty thousand in prison. Fifty thousand children each year are taken into care and there are 100,000 in old people's homes.†

So many people in so many institutions.

I think now of the two old ladies who lived contented lives, at peace with the world, in a wooden shed at the corner of a field near Hemel Hempstead. Officialdom, with the most unimpeachable of motives, obtained a removal order under the National Assistance Act since they would not voluntarily leave their 12 feet by 7 feet hut. The old ladies were moved to an institution and died.

I remember meeting, in the mountainous land to the north of Glasgow, an elderly man who was on the run from an Old People's Home. He had been happily living in a shed which he owned, halfway up the mountain. Conditions there were appalling – enough to strike alarm into the heart of the most sanguine Health Inspector. However, the location was very beautiful and he was happy there.

There came the day that it was decided that his remaining there was a hazard to his health and 'in his own interests' he was taken away to an Old People's Home. It was one of the nicest places – not one of those vast deserted workhouses which sleep hundreds, but a small custom built Old People's Home with central heating.

But of course it was not *his* place. Things went wrong from the start. Used to a lifetime of solitude he found it extremely distressing to have to share a bedroom with another man who muttered in his sleep. On the third day, now well fed but desperate, he escaped. He went back to his shed.

A day later, looking from his windows, he observed policemen approaching. Hastily he locked up, climbed out through a back window and went up the mountain and hid. The police broke down the door of his hut in order to search for him. The old man, realising that there was no place for him here, went to a friend's and asked if he could live in her caravan. A few days later he stealthily returned to his hut, feeling that the hue and cry after him now was probably over. But, since the door had been broken in by the police, it had been swinging in the wind and the damage done to the interior by the weather had been exacerbated by the activities of vandals who had stolen much of his gear. The police had not thought to mend the door.

Heartbroken, he returned to his friend and asked whether he could stay indefinitely in hiding in her caravan. Here he created a home similar to the one up the mountain. He was not any longer able to draw his pension, but he did odd jobs for her which earned him enough money to be kept alive. Yet his was the life of a fugitive.

I asked him whether he would like me to take up his cause by contacting local officials or even writing a newspaper article about him. It seems to me to be important that a British citizen should have the right to grow ill, live, die, sink, swim, in his own place *even* if it is a hazard to his age or health. This seems to me more important than the State's phoney and expensive loving which results in putting him in a centrally heated Home. The old man was, however, of the opinion that any action which brought his present whereabouts to the notice of the authorities or reminded them of his case would have an unfortunate ending; he would be taken back to the institution.

Our spending on our various institutions might strike many strangers as quite extraordinary.

It costs £840 to keep a man in prison for a year.

It can cost £884 to keep him in psychiatric hospital for a year.

It costs up to £884 to keep a child in care of the State.

It costs £676 to keep an old person in an Old People's Home, or £1,200 in a geriatric ward.

The price of keeping so many people in so many institutions is almost incredible, for there are literally hundreds of thousands of people in them. The cost runs to many scores of millions. It is we all who pay. And the answer is a perfectly clear one. In perhaps as many as half of all such cases, such people need not have been in an institution. Instead they could have been housed at the cost of a few pounds a week in small permissive hostels such as I have described in this book. One day the public will see that this is put right because of the incredible expense if not from compassion.

It is always a sobering and humbling experience for me as a writer concerned with the state of the society we inhabit to meet those who are engaged at grass roots level in trying to help, or effect change. Their contributions seem so much more immediate and so much more tangible. I feel admiration and awe when confronted by Tom Gifford, Jim Horne and many others of whom I write in this book. But, when I have asked whether I myself might participate in soup-runs, fund-raising, the running of a hostel, the advice I have been given has been, 'Get back to your typewriter and tape recorder. It is hard enough to find those who will try to change the social order for the better, but even harder to find those who are capable of telling the general public what is going on.'

The country, so such people usually continue, is a democracy, but the information available to its people is of a very trivial and inadequate nature. There is need for informative and campaigning journalism in these times. Shelley used that fine phrase of writers, 'The unacknowledged legislators of mankind', and I have always felt that in these words were contained perhaps the highest aspirations that a writer can have. Also, I suppose, the point could be made that each person should do what *he* is best at in trying to bring about the just society.

Objectivity is an important thing and so it is necessary to stand back even though one's instinct may be to rush in. The ethical maps of the future are drawn by writers, visionaries, philosophers and religious people. However, the failure of most of today's writers must be mentioned. Most contemporary writers do not think in anything other than trivial terms – our failure to indulge in any serious thinking about the nature of the society we live in is sad indeed.

In one sense all writing except technical writing must be about ethics in the sense that all writing implicitly if not explicitly identifies certain things and actions as good and other things and actions as bad. In the realm of human relationships writers are still at the forefront, exploring the morality of the relationships

149

of human beings to one another and redefining the ethics of our lives.

It is with the wider field, the relationship of the individual to the State, that I see little preoccupation in writers. Especially on television, the newest and most challenging medium for the writer today, it is possible to see plenty of current affairs programmes and news items very immediately reflecting the world we live in. But it is possible to sit through play after play after play and find them no more concerned with the thrilling issues of how a rich nation like ours can bring the just society into being than were the confectioners of the decadent court of Louis XIV.

The presence of a large coloured minority in our midst; the erosion of civil rights; abortion; homosexuality; lesbianism; sexual advice for the unmarried; the drop-out of hundreds of thousands of youngsters into hippydom and of their elders into the down and out world; the decline of the church; drugs, our attitude to South Africa; strikes; the non-role of royalty; the alleged discovery of a new sexuality; space travel; the pollution of our environment; the starving third world and its exploitation; the increasing powers of the police and mass institutionalisation of citizens; it is possible to sit through night after night of television plays during which these subjects are curiously absent.

One question I have been asking myself, in writing this book is, How much is this country, which pretends to be Christian, really Christian at all? Certainly the reaction of the State to its failures corresponds to what is taught in the Old Testament, the idea of retribution, the idea of the jealous God. It seems to me that many of the ways that the State deals with those of its citizens who have got into a mess have not advanced beyond that Old Testament attitude. It is as if those who make and administer our laws and our services have not entirely understood, yet, the implications of the teachings of Christ on which our civilisation is allegedly based, have not understood that compassion and forgiveness is the Christian answer to failure, not violence.

Oscar Wilde once said; 'As one reads history . . . one is absolutely sickened, not by the crimes that the wicked have committed, but by the punishments that the good have inflicted.' I cannot see from the evidence available that our civilisation has in many respects attained a Christian attitude to its citizens. I would like to go further and ask what exactly is the role of the churches today? To ask this question is not, I think, invidious since they do set themselves up as our official consciences. What role could there be for the vast network of churches that we have in Britain, scattered through the length and breadth of the land, almost all of them empty for nearly all of the time, and nearly all of them almost empty also on Sundays.

What role could there be for the parsons, now that so much of the traditional work of the clergy has been usurped by the Welfare State. It is partly the churches' fault for allowing this to happen. And the State would be more effective with their help.

One role of the local parson in the past was to act as ombudsman and protective father to his congregation. That function has now been largely abandoned. Homeless families asking whether they may sleep in churches have been turned away and the church doors locked against them. Tramps and beggars, those whom Christ especially singled out as being in need of help, are frequently refused admission to our churches to spend the night in their warmth.

Yet the churches, with their vast resources, and huge areas of roof space, with their vast numbers of personnel and money, could be a new force in our land, a force of humanity and joy which could breathe that feeling of life and compassion into our Welfare State which has so often been lost in bureaucratic bumbling. The clergy should come down from their genteel fortresses.

The existing reaction of a few (mostly non-churchmen) points to the way that they should go. The most useful churches now are those which have opened their crypts to down and outs and in other ways involved themselves in contributing to the happiness of human beings. Why are the churches no longer the centre of entertainment, and life blood of their communities? Why have such things been hived off to the cinemas and Bingo Halls?

In late Victorian times the Salvation Army provided the sort of architecture that their congregation felt at home in, the sort of music that they felt at home with. And above all, they involved themselves with trying to help the homeless, the down and outs, and the needy. Can it be that the rest of the church has lost its soul in exchange for a mass of stones and mortar?

The churches are indeed often lovely. I myself have spent many happy hours playing the organ in these places. But they are too beautiful. Their beauty suggests that nothing is wrong. Christ told of the stultifying effect of too much property on the human soul. The church has too much property; its spirit is being tapped at root.

As many as one in three of the churches should be kept. Others should be sold or adapted for services to the community; as homes, hotels, inns, places of entertainment, museums, concert halls, theatres, building sites; or sold and the money used to set up hostels for the needy. The same holds good for the church-yards. The dead too must be moved – or rather, their headstones. It is an incredible selfishness which I am sure that the dead cannot really subscribe to, that they should take up so much space in the centre of our cities – space that could be used for pleasure parks or playing fields.

The answer to many of the ills described in this book, so I believe, lies in this: the provision of small permissive hostels with a resident father figure. There are now a few hundred of such places in Britain – but there is a need for thousands. And I am sorry to say that all too frequently one hears of the residents of some street or other banding together to try to force a court of inquiry into such few friendly hostels as there are, to force them to close down. Hardly a week goes by without attempts to close such places.

Some Rowton Houses are closing or have closed – and each sleeps many hundreds of men. Two hundred and fifty Spikes have closed down in the past twenty years.

I should like to see a place in every few streets, where those who are down and out, those who in any way cannot cope, can be taken in – a house of hospitality. These places would be like the best small hostels I have described in this book. I would like to see the role of the Warden, the man who looks after this place, become one of the most respected professions in the land. Such people would be carefully sought for.

'The providing of more small permissive hostels,' so Kenneth Stoneley of the NAVH tells me, 'could be made a lot easier by similar legislation to that in the Criminal Justice Act 1967. This provides that the Home Office may underpin places allocated by hostels to ex-prisoners. Many hostels have sprung up and undoubtedly an increasing number of beds are provided for the ex-prisoner; an artificial extended family, a social point of reference in which they can find themselves and learn to be happy.

'What I would like to see now is legislation enabling the government to underwrite places in hostels for other misfits as well; the alcoholics, those who are dependent on drugs, eneuritics, sexual deviants, the mentally disturbed down and outs and the rest. It seems to me that it is wrong to single out just those who have been in prison, for help. We all have our problems although we've not all been in prison.'

But other experienced people have told me that there is a vast

152

need also for hostels that don't take State money – because the State then inevitably seems to insist on regulations that spoil their free and easy nature.

People in a Cardiff Street protested at a proposal to open a hostel for discharged prisoners. Eighty-six people signed a petition that said that they feared for the safety of young children and girls. And that they would live in fear of burglaries. They also were sanctimonious enough to express concern for the safety of Judges who stay nearby when sitting at Assizes. 'Who knows, one of these discharged prisoners may have been sentenced by these judges and have violent intent,' said one of the objection committee. But if nobody makes sacrifices, it seem unlikely that there will ever be an end to the sort of things I have shown in this book. I have always felt that a crash course for magistrates, judges, and other law-keepers and officials of one week as inmates of a Home for the Homeless and one week in prison before they assume office would be most valuable. Probably it would be good for judges once in a while, to meet on a social level, those human wrecks who have spent long years in gaol.

A hostel for men who are incapable of holding a regular job, to be set up by a special After-Care Trust financed by the Carnegie Trust, was unable to be opened because of objections from neighbours. Christian Action have faced court inquiries into their hostel for inebriate persons in the East End of London. The Simon Community has again and again suffered from such inquiries, which have sometimes forced their hostels to close.

Such things belong in that same tragic area as what happened to recent attempts to found an adventure playground in Newport. These were described by neighbours in the Press as a 'Dirty Old Man's Charter' since it was said that an adventure playground would encourage old men to look up schoolgirls' skirts!

And should we change the system?

Could the Welfare State work any better under any other political system?

There are many who will say that the particular things that go wrong under this system would be just as likely to go wrong under any other political system.

A system has not yet been devised, so many people will say, in which those who are socially abnormal are not punished in some way.

The bureaucratic deadly virtues, so such people say, will

153

flourish just as well under any system so far devised or likely to be devised.

Does not socialism, though, come closer to the acceptance of other people as human beings, rather than as digits in an authoritarian regime?

Well, not entirely. In their reactions to new threats to human dignity, such as the threat posed by the despoiling of our environment, socialists seem to lag behind the other parties. Also, it was a socialist government, that, after the last war, told the BBC not to put on programmes which romanticised tramps or nonworkers or pictured them in an idealistic light.

These things can be said against socialism. But it remains in my mind that the National Assistance Act, which the present Welfare State is built on, was a product of socialism. That there should henceforth be freedom from want. That the only criterion for help should be need. That there should no more be discrimination against any person on grounds of race, colour, or creed. . . . In this concept can be found, I think, the noblest piece of legislation of this century, perhaps, of the whole of history. This was a piece of socialist legislation.

I still hope and believe that there lies embedded in socialist doctrine a caring for people, all people, that runs directly contrary to the sort of inflexible authoritarianism which so many of the organisations mentioned in this book are bedevilled by.

The Welfare State was a humane structure erected over the smouldering bones of a not yet extinct Poor Law.

Obviously, one cannot immediately effect legislation which will immediately change the hearts of people who have grown up in a very different tradition.

I would prefer to feel that those ways in which the Welfare State has so far failed are the product of those old authoritarian elements which have lingered on from the bad old days. I hope that as the changing years replace old personnel with new, that we may come to see a complex of social services that are truly caring.

Yet I am often filled with alarm. For the increase in authoritarianism is becoming acute. Recently 150 children were given a tea-party in a quiet Brighton Street. Wearing paper hats they were tucking into tea and cakes and jellies and cream buns and fancy pastries.

Unfortunately the people who organised the party had not been given permission for the street party. The result was that five police cars closed in, the street was cleared and twenty of the organisers wearing their paper hats were rounded up and taken to the police station.

What an extraordinarily sad example this is, it seems to me, of the way we are becoming victims of authoritarianism. Who owns the streets? Who owns the parks? Again and again the State applies an incredible set of authoritarian rules which prevent us acting spontaneously and doing the things we want to.

Yet the State is only our creation. We must learn to bust it.

Can there be some deeper psychological reason for the thrusting into the role of madman, criminal, or dosser, those who did not start as these things? I know little of psychiatry but it seems to me that there may be a fruitful field for enquiry here.

Most systems of psychiatry accept that we are divided into three parts – the super-ego (the repository of paternal wisdom and the wise and also unwise laws of society): the ego; and the Id (those parts of us that act exclusively on appetite and instinct). Each man in attaining maturity must learn to live with the first and to control the last, although about precisely how much this should be done there is a certain amount of disagreement.

It seems to me that too many of us project the same sort of structure on society. Because of our own make-up we want to believe that there are all-wise persons bringing to bear on our lives their traditional wisdom. Many also desire an all-wise God. Hence the hero worship and putting on a pedestal of establishment figures. Similarly, many of us need to feel that those licentious and wild elements in us of which we are ourselves afraid are also paralleled in society as a whole, and must similarly be put down at any rate in part.

And so we allot to many pathetic people the role of criminal or scapegoat – asking them to play fantasy parts in our own internal dramas.

Sexual envy is an important part of this. As people grow older and their sexual prowess begins to fade, it is inevitable that they feel jealous of the young in whom sexuality is at its height.

They then often come to identify sexuality not as the all-powerful and good thing which the young feel it to be, but rather like the weasels and stoats in Toad of Toad Hall – the thing which will swarm in and destroy their equilibrium.

So the young are resented for their sexuality and the amazingly punititive sentences which are sometimes meted out to the young and sexy spring from this tragic lack of sophistication on the part of our older establishment figures.

This sort of projection exists at all sorts of levels in society at the moment. The basic way to fight it is to try to relate to all other people as humans like us, rather than conniving at the existing system of treating some of them as wise or unwise parents, and others as delinquent children.

I have been touring with an organisation which has now control of something like forty Hostels similar to those which I advocate in this book. Together with Tom Gifford I have been showing my film of 'Edna' and lecturing and calling for recruits after it.

It has been a moving experience. Unlike so many charities, the aim of the Cyrenians is not primarily to raise money. Rather, it is to gain recruits to live for a year in a small charitable hostel, helping the residents to claim their rights and live as citizens of Britain rather than, as previously, helpless beings herded in a gutter.

In the towns we speak in, when I can, I stay in a Cyrenian hostel, eating and sleeping with those for whom previously the only possible home was the street or the common lodging house.

They are impressive places. When staying there I have talked to many people who until the Cyrenians came along, were Down and Out.

I did not realise, until I did this, just how extensive are the blacklists operated by the larger type of common lodging houses. I have learnt of pathetic creatures being thrown out from charitable hostels of the more conventional type into the street. And occasionally dying there.

I myself have been on a 'squat' with the Cyrenians in empty buildings in Brighton in order to draw attention to the inadequacy of the old Spike in that town to cater for those for whom it was designed. I have seen the destruction by Local Authorities of huge lodging houses, making scores and sometimes hundreds of men homeless.

I have already explained how the National Assistance Board (later the DHSS), given the duty in the National Assistance Act (1948) to provide temporary accommodation for those of an unsettled way of living and to help them to lead a more settled life has totally ignored this duty. When the Act was passed they had in their possession something like three hundred Spikes. True, they were old-fashioned – but they existed as they had been de-designed to do, a day's walk apart, and they formed a network of buildings which could have been of great use in helping solve the Down and Out problem.

Nothing of the sort occurred. Since that time the number has been whittled down until now they have left only about twenty.

Vast organisations like Rowton Houses have continued to close and the Salvation Army also has closed kiphouses which it has replaced with buildings of higher standard – too high a standard for many dossers.

There is room for hope though. While most Local Authorities continue to slam the door in the face of any organisation who try to provide small hostels for the homeless, some have collaborated.

The most notable has been Hammersmith, in whose Borough a vast Rowton House was closing. They now finance six houses run by the Cyrenians and the St Mungo Community – and let us hope that this will be the precedent for other similar operations.

The press conference that launched my film *Edna, the Inebriate Woman*, was held at the new Christian Action Hostel for Homeless Women, in Greek Street, London.

At this press conference one of the inhabitants, Maureen MacMahon, read the following poem:

> 'Have you ever had nowhere to stay?
> Nowhere your weary body can lay?
> You walk and walk and get no place,
> And all around there's no friendly face,
> You reach a railway station and think,
> I'll sit awhile and have a drink,
> But a policeman soon comes into view,
> In a rather harsh voice he says "Hey you!
> Move on! Move on! You can't stay!"
>
> So wearily you go on your way.'
> You feel a longing to be dead,
> You only want to rest your head,
> You wonder grimly if you were
> In your grave, you could stay there,
> Or would a policeman soon appear,
> Saying: "Move on! Move! You can't stop here!" '

It was not so long after this that Maureen died by her own hand. She left behind her a second poem, even more moving perhaps than the first:

'I feel myself slipping away,
Nothing more can make me stay,
I must destroy the physical me,
So that my spirit can be free.
I must go, so that I'll find,
My sanity, and peace of mind.

The memory of the me that lingers on,
Must not be a sad or unhappy one,
I am not worthy of your sorrow.
I could not live to face tomorrow,
My heart is full of love for you,
And sadness for my failure too.'

If the reader is in agreement with what is said in this book, he should speak with his friends about the idea that our society is becoming harder and harder for people to live in, and that those who are unable to cope are often not so much helped as given a kick in the crutch.

If he would like to be involved in trying to rescue people from the Down and Out world and see them instead helped back to their feet in small permissive hostels, he should write to one of the organisations listed at the end of this book, asking how he can help.

If the organisation has no representative in his particular town or area, he should consider joining with others in the setting up of such a place himself. The life can be a worthwhile one and it does not require more than a year from the life of anyone, although many of those who live it say that it is more addictive than alcohol; they become unable to give it up.

Students especially find the life worthwhile. It's a hard life but worth a thousand times more than the senseless struggle of the rat race.

Move on, move on . . .

This seems to be the reality of life for thousands of dossers and down-and-outs in Britain.

'Oh yes, the shades (police) like to have a clean beat,' one tells me.

And yet down-and-outs possess many Christ-like virtues. They take no thought for the morrow, lay up no worldly goods.

It is time we stopped persecuting them and asked what we can learn from them.

Many of the people in this book are people to whom violence has been done. And to a certain extent this has kept them, though adult in physical appearance, at the stage of development of children.

If I behave unjustly to a child he will sulk and say, 'I hate you'. But what he is really saying is, 'Please love me'. A wise parent or schoolmaster realises this, and that a fit of the sulks is only a claim for love.

But when a grown adult gets into that state and sulks and says, 'Fuck society, put me back in the nick, at any rate that's warm,' etc, etc, we take this at its face value. Perhaps because these are people with the minds of children but without a child's winning appearance to help us to care for them.

Yet, help we must and care we must. Because this class of person is growing. More and more people each year are going into care, and, despite drastic pruning, entry into psychiatric hospitals remains roughly constant. More people are going into the courts, into homes for juveniles and into prison – and especially amongst teenagers.

The flood of homeless teenagers who seem unable to cope with society is becoming so great that it now constitutes one-third of all the NAVH placements. And this is a grave sign. Many of course will find a happier orientation in life when they 'settle down'. But the numbers are too great for us to write off the danger so easily.

And, if we don't learn better how to cope with the rejects of Britain they will continue to grow in numbers – till that point that they constitute a population numbering not just scores of thousands but hundreds of thousands.

NOTES

Critics of 'Edna' and 'Down and Out'

It is not customary for writers to reply to their critics: a dignified silence is considered more appropriate.

I think this a pity. A year or so passes between the appearance of a book in hardcover and soft cover, and this passing of a year before the reappearance of his book gives a writer the chance to mull over what he has written and to reply to the more interesting points raised by his critics.

Those writers who don't reply do wrong. A book is an edifice of ideas set up in the market place by its author in the hope that it will (by however small a degree) alter the status quo. The writer has stood up and made a statement. How cowardly it is and how irresponsible, it seems to me, if, having made such a statement and provoked discussion, the author then retires from view.

And, so I'd like to say something here about the reaction of the critics to the first appearance of *Down and Out in Britain*, and also to my play *Edna, the Inebriate Woman* which came out simultaneously, and was about the same subject.

An interesting point is that few appeared able to absorb the basic point that the book was making: that our State is needlessly cruel. One man, a book reviewer for Radio London, even believed it to be a work of fiction!

Many critics and other readers, so it seems to me, adopted a whole succession of intellectual alibis as smoke screens (subconsciously) rather than to accept this, or face it.

However, the *Evening Standard*, in their leader following publication of the book and showing of the play, got it right; 'A frightening personal dossier on what it is like for so many people to live beyond the reach of society's day-to-day rescue services. At this level of degradation, the Welfare State, in Mr Sandford's words, is "A ladder from which the last few rungs seem broken or missing".'

Alan Brien in the *Sunday Times* was also right: 'The surprising thing about Edna was not that she drank, but that she was not perpetually drunk. In a society where alcohol is still the opiate of the successful why should not those who society brands as failures, as the dregs, drain the dregs of its bottles?

'We provide for those dying on their backs, why not for those dying on their feet?'

D. A. N. Jones, writing in the *New Statesman* and *Radio Times*, was not able to take the message quite so straight. He mentions how the recent Greve Report, *Homelessness in London*, commended my newspaper reports and my 'Cathy'. So too, he says, did the U.N.-inspired report *Socially deprived families in Britain*, in which Robert Holman 'urged social workers to learn how to manipulate the mass media in the way Sandford had done, so that public opinion could be changed and more money made available to benefit the "socially deprived".'

'The book,' D. A. N. Jones goes on, 'is primarily a sermon, urging more Christian love and self-sacrifice, illustrated by properly lurid anecdotes about cases of hardship which need to be alleviated. . . . The criticisms of government and municipal welfare agencies may be useful, provided that the workers in these departments don't get discouraged and resentful.'

But he is unable to accept my view of the 'man-mad fifteen year old girl'. A number of other critics single her out from the book, so it's perhaps worth saying a few words here about her. 'Later,' says D. A. N. Jones, 'there is a great deal of blame for cruel policemen and magistrates. For instance, a very promiscuous and violent fifteen-year-old girl was brought before a court by her mother, after she had tried to commit suicide. She was sent to a Remand Home for a report. Sandford suggests that "in her obvious rejection of all the bourgeois standards of the place where she grew up, this girl, albeit violent, was in fact more adult than those who sentenced her".'

D. A. N. Jones comments; 'There are many snap judgements like this; some sound like parodies by Peter Simple.'

There is a basic misunderstanding here, I think, so perhaps I should say a few words about it. In the book I say 'may it not be that . . . the girl was more adult than those who sentenced her?' I still feel this.

I feel that the word 'adult' hardly can be applied to a court who, a roomful of rejecting establishment figures, are prepared to sit back and hear a girl's mother dismiss her daughter in the cruel way that she did.

I wrote a letter to *New Society* about this. 'The girl was having sex at an age when public opinion says that she shouldn't. But why shouldn't she? To be man-mad is acceptable it seems at the age of 19 in Hollywood or Chelsea, but not at the age of 15 in a British hick town. James Bond was clearly girl-mad and is a national hero, but just look how we punish his youthful female admirers. Was not this girl's bravado, and her later violence and attempt at suicide a pathetic reaction to this denial of her needs as a person? She may not have gone far along the road to adulthood, but surely she was further than those who thought the answer was to humiliate her in public and then shut her up?

'I can't accept that this girl was more sick than the adults in her life. Not sick at all, perhaps, till those from the adult world, with whom she came into contact made her so. It was our sickness she caught.'

One of the more curious critiques at this time came also from D. A.

N. Jones, in the *Radio Times*. Here Jones warned viewers, before *Edna* was even seen, that he 'did not think it would work.' He himself hadn't actually seen either script or film at this point, which goes to show how ably the sixth sense has been cultivated by some critics.

I wrote a letter to the editor of the *Radio Times* which amused me at the time: 'It may be that the editor of *Radio Times* planned to intrigue and attract viewers by this perversity, and in the world of the super-sell, perhaps a little fog may win viewers.' I went on to say that I looked forward to further announcements in this vein which could perhaps be referred to as 'the drooping sell'. For 'Coronation Street' I suggested that the billing should be 'doubt whether many will consider it worth watching'. For the Christmas programmes, my suggestion was 'general effect will be depressing'; and for the news, 'mostly lies'.

Edward Lucie-Smith in the *New Statesman* wrote: 'Naturally Jeremy Sandford's latest effort, "Edna, the Inebriate Woman" aroused one's expectations.

'Expectations of what? Chiefly, I think of a very generous and human compassion linked to a detailed knowledge of the milieu which was depicted.'

Clive James in *The Listener* said 'Our society produces damaged people where previous societies produced corpses. It's an improvement, but not one with which a sensitive man can rest content. Mr Sandford tries to rub our noses in reality, but the truth is, the reality is worse.'

And he goes on to say, about my advocacy of hostels, 'It is lethal to suggest that things could be fixed by asking the dis-adapted back in amongst us. In amongst us is where they got the way they are. What we have to do is find a way to stop churning them out.'

I replied as follows; 'Estimates are that there are 2,000 people actually sleeping out in the cold tonight in London alone. There are thousands sleeping rough in the rest of Britain. Many thousands need-lessly in psychiatric hospital and lodging houses and prison. This is the horrible actual situation, and I can't believe that Clive James feels that we shouldn't ask them back amongst us. Surely any action is desirable which gets a decent roof over their heads? And if Clive James doesn't feel that now, surely he will when those sleeping rough begin to die when the cold weather really begins?

'I suggest that we *must* ask these tragic people back in amongst us. Once we've done that we can consider the long term question.'

Confusion was caused here, I believe, by the phrase 'in amongst us'. I think the dossers get the way they are because they're not amongst us – they're away in institutions or out in the night. To ask them into a small permissive hostel would be my way of really asking them 'back amongst us' – something which few people, so far, have ever done.

One of the most useful printed comments came as might have been expected from Des Wilson. He wrote as follows in *The Observer*; 'Peggy, the down and out, makes her television debut on Thursday – a fleeting appearance in Jeremy Sandford's BBC TV play about homeless women, "Edna, the Inebriate Woman". Peggy would have liked them to make a film about her – because it could help somebody else.

'I was the eldest child of four. Even as a baby my mother didn't want me. She was going to put me in Dr Barnados, but Gran wouldn't let her. Gran brought me up till she died. Then at six I went to live with Mum. Even in those days I was always running away. The police used to find me and I wouldn't know my name. I used to wander for miles.

'It was horrible going back home after Gran died. I always felt terribly unwanted. Mum used to hit me over anything. When I was eight she decided I would have to stay home from school to do the housework and look after my four-year-old brother. The school board kept writing, but she just burned the letters. I came up before the Juvenile Court and went away on two weeks remand. They asked my mother why I didn't go to school. D'you know what she said? "I can't make her go – she's beyond my control." And I got three years in Approved School.'

'I've been in and out of hospital and prison ever since. Every hospital I've ever been in, except Broadmoor, I've run away from – at Broadmoor you don't stand a chance. (Once I found a ladder and climbed over the wall, but I was so afraid of the dogs I rang the admission bell and said, "Here I am.")'

Peggy on alcoholism: 'My father was an alcoholic. For years I drank very heavily but it didn't really help. I used to drink a bottle of cheap wine at night.'

Peggy on Security: 'I like a little bit of security. When things get too much for me I go down to the police station and say I've done so and so. Then I get sent to prison.'

And Peggy on the Welfare State: 'If I had the time ever again, it would be difficult not to do a repeat performance. No one has been any real help to me. Their treatment seems to have had a lasting effect.'

Peggy, a big woman – well over sixteen stone – who talks colourfully, even when to the press, was thrilled about being an extra in Jeremy Sandford's play. For the first and only time in her life, she was part of a thing that was being created and that would be taken notice of. After nearly thirty years as one of Britain's forgotten, she and her kind – female tramps – were temporarily to be remembered, sympathised with, and perhaps even helped.

But sadly, she will never see the programme. Soon after it was finished she was found dead in a discharged prisoners' hospital at Holloway. She had taken an overdose of sleeping tablets. She was thirty-seven.

It may have been an accident. However, her hands and wrists were covered with the traces of deep wounds caused by suicide attempts.

'I must have taken overdoses on dozens of different occasions,' she had said. 'I don't only overdose. I slit myself with bits of glass, I break milk bottles and eat bits of the glass.'

So maybe she had deliberately confirmed her prediction; 'I'll die quite soon and make a vacancy for someone else.'

An interesting letter came from Louis Gillain in Portsmouth, in the

Radio Times. 'In his excellent, if mild and polite, depiction of the society in which I was born and rightfully belong, Jeremy Sandford rather evades the point.

' . . . I was born in a workhouse and, apart from a few brief attempts to join respectable society, remained an illiterate vagrant till 1947. Even the war-time army wouldn't have me.

'The fact is, the degree of enjoyment and suffering is proportionately the same in all stratas of society. There are as many laughs and sighs in the gutter as elsewhere. So with inebriation: it is the sport of all ranks.

' . . . Your problem is that the lowest ranks must be there or else there is no one against whom you – the respectable – can measure your own supposed superiority. This is all you have by way of reward for living.

'It is not a culpable fault is it, your inheritance. . . .

'This is due mainly to your formal system of education which develops your retentive and calculative faculties at the expense of your insight, which is all but atrophied, and particularly noticeable among your erudite and academicians.'

I wrote back agreeing with this letter. I said: 'I am sure that there is a self-perpetuating streak in our society, designed to keep the poor always with us, and it is important for us all to be aware of this and fight against it both in ourselves and in society.

' . . . The most valued mail received by me has been that from social workers and others in the field of charity.'

A parson, member of a committee which seeks to found a hostel such as shown in 'Edna' and described in *Down and Out*, wrote: 'The experience of seeing the play has sharpened and concentrated the awareness of many committee members . . . and others have written to me saying they feel that "Edna" will increase the public's awareness of the problems of the homeless single inadequate person, as "Cathy" did for the homeless family.'

I answered various other correspondents in *Radio Times* as follows: 'My plays are meant to be social not literary documents, and the primary aim is not to cheer people but to jog them into thinking and action – though of course if a play is not interesting to watch, they will switch it off.

'I was saddened by the correspondent who suggested that it was done for gain. The amount of research necessary for writing a play like this swallows up more than the fee, since it must be first hand research carried out in fields where there are few written sources.

'The best endorsement for *Edna* for me comes not from letters but from the fact that Christian Action and the Cyrenians, organisers of hostels like that in the play, tell me that the phone has been constantly ringing since with offers of help.

'That puts into perspective for me the people who write letters signed "Disgusted". There are thousands of people sleeping out in the cold tonight in Britain. Let's get them under a roof – and then write letters.'

The review in *Ink* was in many ways the best.

Jim Donovan wrote: 'The essence of this book is contained in the charge that "those who fail we do not always help, instead we punish them".

'Above all else this book is a serious piece of social documentation and a book that someone somewhere just had to write . . . this time Jeremy Sandford is holding up yet another image of our society and if we accept that truth is beautiful then we must admit that the picture is far from pretty. If the phrase "descending into the bilges of our society" sounds a little too heroic for those readers who distrust the antics of middle class slummers and other social skin divers, then I would ask them to be patient; Mr Sandford's tales about old ladies subsisting on a diet of metal polish, butties and surgical spirit may raise eyebrows around the dinner tables of suburbia, but let us hope that his probe into the causes behind these symptoms will raise some action.'

Geoffrey Parkinson, writing in *New Society*, says; 'The book finally makes one point very clearly: people in power have got to realise the suffering of the powerless, even when the powerless cannot always fit themselves into a "good cause" mould'.

However, he goes on to say 'I cannot help feeling that, when in regions of social uncertainty, Jeremy Sandford tends to either slightly fictionalise problems or over-idealise people with problems'.

As example of this he says that I link the down and out life 'with the ideals of Christianity, which is about as true as saying that the survivors from a sinking ship jump into the water for the pleasure of the swim'.

I cannot agree with this. I made the mistake of half emptying a hall where I was recently lecturing in Scotland by referring to Christ as a 'propertyless vagrant'. I think that Parkinson may be suffering from the same mental block as those worthy people who then sprang to their feet and left the hall.

The ideal society should embrace all forms of life in its citizenry and provide for them.

I believe that all of those who are down and out are victims. But this doesn't mean that I am saying that some of those who lead the life of vagrants would not continue to do so even if society were so designed that they needn't. The vagrant's life has attractions and the difference would be that, if this ever happened, those who followed Christ's precepts in this manner would be happy in their elected life, not unhappy.

As another example, Parkinson mentions the fifteen-year-old girl who I referred to above.

He comments: 'Discounting slick sociology, from any point of view this girl was sick, and though it may surprise Sandford some Remand Homes are quite "like Butlins".'

Well, I have said my feelings about this girl. I have seen Remand Homes and Approved schools and I haven't liked them. But this is not the point I was making. What I was saying was that the girl was more adult than those who sentenced her, and for the court to connive in this public dismissal by her mother was shocking.

The most critical of all the reviews I got came from Mary Holland in

The Observer. She felt that *Edna* and *Cathy* failed because they 'made no meaningful assault on the fundamental causes of the problem'. I answered her in a letter: 'My own feeling was that the public were so ignorant of the plight of blameless homeless families that I must get them aware that the problem exists before they were ready to look beyond to the "fundamental causes".'

'It is only possible to do so much in one play and *Cathy* achieved what I wanted it to do: to show that the State still punishes innocent families. Until that proposition was entirely accepted, I felt that consideration of the 'fundamental causes' might put off the general public, rather than the reverse.

'One can't do more than a certain number of things at one time: for instance in her review, Mary Holland doesn't go into the fundamental causes of so much bad television. She could have written of the absurd BBC rule that productions must be in colour even when they are more suited to black and white – a rule which results in a vast expense of money and time. . . .

'*Cathy* contained no solution, but when I came to write *Edna* I decided to embody in the play what seemed to me to be the solution. It is not a very original one: the government's report on the Habitual Drunken Offender suggests that the small permissive hostel is the answer. The Criminal Justice Act and RAP (Radical Alternatives to Prison) are two other products of informed opinion which advocate this. What stands in the way is the hostility of the public to having such things in their street and the shortage of funds. I wrote *Edna* to change this.

'I don't hold out the small permissive hostel as the answer to all social ills, as Mary Holland suggests. Of course it isn't. But I do think it is the answer to this one. Thousands of people will be sleeping in the open in Britain tonight, as on every night. Let's try to get a roof over their heads: in the morning there's time to get to the fundamental causes.'

One of the reviews which perhaps understandably I felt to be important was in *Social Action*, the journal of the Simon Community.

There, John Hill wrote: 'With like passion, Jeremy Sandford and Anton Wallich Clifford (the director of Simon Community) hit out against the neglect of socially inadequate people.

' . . . Both men are playing vital roles in a crisis too large to describe within limits, boundaries or horizons. They are not, like too many of us, conveniently blind to the disgusting and utterly demoralising shame which one man can bring upon another. They can, and do, identify with a heap of rags in a doorway, the head lolled to one side – living ashes of a murder committed by you, I and Britain – the Christian hypocrite which with unforgivable audacity and bland naivete asks to be called democracy.

' . . . Sandford, garbed in shabby greatcoat and bearded, lived in the filthy heart of Skid Row for the time needed to form his compelling book.

'Jeremy Sandford and Anton Wallich-Clifford are just two among the many dedicated men and women in this country who are attacking a crisis which they can hope only, at best, to diminish.'

These are flattering words. If only a quarter of them were true, I would be happy.

The Vagrancy Act

One of the most senseless of all our laws is the Vagrancy Act, under which dossers and vagrants are still imprisoned to this day. It goes: AN ACT for the Punishment of Idle and Disorderly Persons, and Rogues and Vagabonds, in that part of *Great Britain* called *England*. (June 21st, 1824)

... Be it ... enacted that every person being able wholly or in part to maintain himself or herself, or his or her family, by work or by other means, and wilfully refusing or neglecting so to do by which refusal or neglect he or she, or any of his or her family whom he or she may be legally bound to maintain, shall have become chargeable to any Parish, Township or Place ... every petty chapman or pedlar wandering abroad and trading, without being duly licensed, or otherwise author- ised by law; every common prostitute wandering in the public streets or public highways, or in any place of public resort, and behaving in a riotous or indecent manner; and every person wandering abroad, or placing himself or herself in any public place, street, highway, court, or passage, to beg or gather alms, or causing or procuring or encouraging any child or children so to do, shall be deemed an idle and disorderly Person within the true intent and meaning of this Act; and it shall be lawful for any Justice of the Peace to commit such offender (being thereof convicted before him by his own view ...) to the House of Correction there to be kept to hard labour. ...

And it is further enacted that, every Person committing any of the offences herein before mentioned, after having been convicted as an idle and disorderly Person; every Person pretending or professing to tell fortunes, or using any subtle craft, means, or device, by palmistry or otherwise, to deceive and impose on any of His Majesty's subjects; every Person wandering abroad and lodging in any barn or outhouse, or any deserted or unoccupied building, or in the open air, or under a tent, or in any cart or wagon, not having any visible means of subsis- tence, and not giving a good account of himself or herself; every Person wilfully exposing to view in any street, road, highway, or public place, any obscene print, picture or other indecent exhibition; every Person wilfully, openly, lewdly, and obscenely, exposing his person in any street, road, or public highway, or in the view thereof or in any place of public resort with intent to insult any female; every Person wandering abroad and endeavouring by the exposure of wounds or deformities to obtain or gather alms; every Person going abroad as a gatherer or collector of alms, or endeavouring to procure charitable contributions of any nature or kind, under any fraudulent pretence; every Person running away and leaving his wife, or his or her child or children, chargeable, or whereby she or they or any of them shall become chargeable to any Parish, Township, or Place; . . . every Person having in his or her custody or possession any pick-lock, key, crow, jack, bit, or other implement, with intent erroneously to break into any dwelling-house, warehouse, coach-house, stable, or outbuilding . . . every Person being found in or upon any enclosed yard, garden, or area for any unlawful purpose; every suspected Person or reputed thief, frequenting any river, canal, or navigable stream, dock, or basin . . . and every Person apprehended as an idle and disorderly Person, and violently resisting any constable or other police officer apprehending him or her, and being subsequently convicted of the offence for which he or she shall have been so apprehended, shall be deemed a Rogue and Vagabond, within the true intent and meaning of this Act; and it shall be lawful for any Justice of the Peace to commit such offender (being thereof convicted before him by the confession of such offender or by the evidence on oath of one or more credible witness or witnesses) to the House of Correction, there to be kept to hard labour for any time not exceeding three calendar months. . . .

Much of the Establishment's attitude to Down and Outs can be traced back to this Vagrancy Act of 1824. Hard labour is gone. The House of Correction is gone. But Spikes, prison, the dosshouse, and, above all, the attitude remain.

NOTES ON THE TEXT

Sleeping rough, and Days and Nights in the Kiphouse

The nuns with whom I went on the soup run are the Poor Sisters of the Mother of God, from Mayfield Convent, Roehampton Lane, London S.W.15. The soup run is organised by Jim Horne of the St Mungo Community, Home Road, Battersea, London S.W.11. Each night he sends out a different group of people along the embankments and under the arches. He has set up many permissive hostels in different areas in London.

The Simon Community Trust is an organisation which for many years now has sought to help society's misfits, and now, particularly, have turned to homeless families. Their address is: Grange Road, Ramsgate, Kent.

This was Edward Gillespie, at the Lodging House Mission, East Campbell Street, Glasgow.

Christian Action run various hostels and their headquarters is at 104 Newgate Street, London E.C.1. This one, for Homeless Women, was in Lambeth High Street, London S.E.1. Mr Henderson says more about this hostel in his letter to the *Guardian*, 20 May, 1969.

*'No Fixed Abode' by C. Berry and A. Orwin, *British Journal of Psychiatry*, October, 1966.

§Hutchinson, 1963. Tony Parker has written other books with a similar theme, including *Five Women* (Hutchinson, 1965), *People of the Streets* (Cape 1968) and *The Courage of His Convictions* (Hutchinson, 1969).

**The National Association of Voluntary Hostels have their offices at 33 Long Acre, London W.C.2.

These words are quoted from the Christian Action handout 'Faces in the Crowd' (1966) written by Leslie Tuft.

The Cyrenians: Sole Cottages, Crundale, nr Canterbury.

Merfyn Turner's Hostel is at 24 Harburton Road, London N.19. I am drawing partly on a BBC interview he was kind enough to do for me. Merfyn Turner's book about Common Lodging Houses, *Forgotten Men*, was published by the National Council of Social Service, 1960.

This hostel is St Dismas House, Southampton. I have changed the names of the inmates.

Nowhere Else To Go (May, 1970). CARE stands for Cottage and Rural Enterprises.

See HMSO: Prison Report.

This man was Vincent Taylor Brown, aged twenty-three, born in the West Indies. (See *The Times* 21 November, 1969.) Tony Smythe of the NCCL commented on this occasion: 'There are literally dozens of people being held for lengthy periods in prison without having had the charges against them heard. The NCCL is so disturbed that it is taking further action.'

These words were spoken at a Commons Committee considering the Childrens and Young Persons Bill.

Homes for the Homeless

People who wish to know more about Britain's homeless families could consult *London's Homeless* by John Greve (Codicott Press, 1964), *The Homeless Versus Kent County Council* (Solidarity Pamphlet, c/o 53a Westermoreland Road, Bromley, Kent), which describes events at the Hostel for the Homeless at Kinghill in Kent, and my essay in *Cathy Come Home* (Pan, 1967).

This homeless mother living in a Home for the Homeless at Abridge in Essex spoke on Late Night Line-up.

Audrey Harvey was the author of this article in the *New Statesman*, 5 November, 1965. For years she has fought for the homeless and others. She has written *Casualties of the Welfare State* (Fabian Society, 1960) and *Tenants in Danger* (Penguin Special, 1964).

This report appeared in the *Evening Standard*, and the twenty-seven people living in one room were discovered by Shelter. Earlier, Shelter researchers found twenty-two people of mixed races sleeping and living in one big room in the same place – the Dartmouth Road Hostel – and said, 'On one occasion families were sitting for twelve hours in the Welfare Office, before the police were called to eject them. The police took the families to the hostel – much to the annoyance of the Welfare Department.'

Pat Healy of *The Times* reported twenty people comprising five mothers and fifteen children, sleeping 'crammed together in a room 15 by 20 feet in Willesden. Some of the children share beds because there is no space for more beds. The room is the bedroom, sitting-room, and playroom. . . . '

I Know it Was the Place's Fault (Oliphants, 1970).

Children in Care

The Children and Young Persons Act (1969) includes the important provision that there will be no more Approved School orders. The child will be committed to the care of one of twelve regional planning areas. Most Children's Homes will be renamed Community Homes (including the present Remand Homes, Approved Schools and Reception Centres). This, however, will not apply to Borstal, Detention Centres.

The reconviction figures and the accounts of the ex-detention boys are from *Detention Centres: No Right to Speak* (October, 1969), a report by Mary Iles on behalf of the Prison Reform Council.

The Report commissioned by the National Council for Civil Liberties was *Rights of Children and Young Persons* (January, 1968). Their address is, 4 Camden High Street, London N.W.1.

Unmarried Mothers

*This letter is quoted from a pamphlet issued by the National Council for the Unmarried Mother and Her Child. Their address is, 55 Kentish Town Road, London N.W.5.
†*Mother and Baby Homes* (Allen and Unwin 1968).

In 1968, in the *Registrar General's Annual Statistical Review* (Part II: England and Wales) it is reported that there were 69,806, live illegitimate births. The additions of the stillbirth figures and those for Scotland and Northern Ireland gives a larger total. More recent but approximate figures from the *Quarterly Return* for 30 June, 1970 give the total total of 67,100 illegitimate births in England and Wales in 1969.

The ratio of illegitimate to legitimate births seems at last to be falling. In the last quarter of 1967 it was a record 85.9 per thousand. More recently it has been 81 per thousand.

In one table the Registrar General shows that the total births conceived extra-maritally (that is to girls who got married before the birth) as well as to unmarried mothers, was 144,123 in England and Wales, or nearly one out of five of all births in 1967.

In 1967 the total stillbirths per thousand babies was fifteen. But among illegitimate babies the rate was nearly a quarter more – nineteen per thousand babies. In 1968 half as many again illegitimates died on their first day; 9.45 per thousand as against 6.04 legitimate.

†In 1968 14,641 babies were adopted by people other than their parents.
§In the year March 1969–70, 'child illegitimate, mother unable to provide', accounted for 2,709 children being taken into care. (*Children in Care* HMSO 1970.) In the year ending 31 March, 1969, 51,542 children came into care. At that date there were 71,210 children in State care in England and Wales.

Provision of Hostels for Unmarried Mothers. The majority of hostels are provided by the Church of England, but other denominations and the Local Authorities also have quite a number.

Local Health Authorities are empowered to provide services for unmarried mothers directly, and also to assist and supervise those run by voluntary bodies. They generally prefer the second method. They assist with annual block grants or separate *per capita* grants for individual residents.

Income also comes from original foundation grants, money paid by the parents or boy-friends of the girls, subscriptions raised through charity, the maternity grants of the girls, and from sickness benefits and National Assistance. The Homes employ a matron who is usually unqualified, and often there are few other staff. Recruitment is getting harder, and there is a growing lack of those public spirited single women who in previous times, for a small fee, were prepared to devote their lives to running places like these.

Most Homes are run by a committee of local people fairly closely linked to the church that provides them. A way to improve the Homes would be compulsory registration, followed by inspection at a national level. The present situation is that all Homes providing maternity facilities have to be registered under the Nursing Act, but as regards the others the legislation is open to different interpretations, and it is still a matter for each local authority to decide whether or not to register these Homes.

There are now about 110 Mother and Baby Hostels on the books of the National Council for the Unmarried Mother and Her Child.

The present increase in availability of contraception, abortion, and information, will probably eventually put an end to the evils of which I write. What is tragic is that, unless some way is found to speed things up, thousands of girls will continue to go through this sort of experience for many years yet. The address of Mothers in Action, a campaigning organisation, is c/o their Secretary,10 Lady Somerset Road,London N.W.5.
†It is difficult to obtain abortions in many areas: for instance, the London rate is over three and a half times that of Birmingham. The number of abortions notified in Newcastle is almost double that of Leeds a city of similar size.
§Schoolmothers: in 1967 a baby was born to an eleven-year-old, six to twelve-year-olds, thirty to thirteen-year-olds, 194 to fourteen-year-olds, 1,010 to fifteen-year-olds, and 2,650 to sixteen-year-olds. In 1968 the figures were four babies born to twelve-year-olds, twenty-five to thirteen-year-olds, 193 to fourteen-year-olds, 1,083 to fifteen-year-olds, 5,146 to sixteen-year-olds.

†There are 100,000 old folk in Local Authority Residential Accommodation in England alone (Department of Health and Social Security *Annual Report*, 1969, gives the figure 97,475 for 1969). There were 20,820 members of homeless families living in temporary accommodation on 31 December, 1969 (Op. cit., p. 217). During 1969, 177,818 patients were admitted to psychiatric hospital (Op. cit., p. 277). On 31 December, 1969, there were 168,846 psychiatric patients in England (Op. cit., p. 278). For the number in prison, see note to p. 89, and for children in care see note to p.§117.

Hamish Hamilton, 1970. We estimate to spend £53,615,000 on residential accommodation for the old in 1970–71, and £2,516,000 on homeless families in England alone. (Department of Health and Social Security *Annual Report*, 1969, p. 231.) A psychiatric in-patient cost up to £16 per week in 1968–69.

Recommended Organisations

The Cyrenians; director Tom Gifford; National Headquarters at Sole Cottages, Crundale, near Canterbury.

The Simon Community; director Anton Wallich-Clifford; head office, Grange Road, Ramsgate, Kent.

The St Mungos Community: director Jim Horne; Headquarters, Home Road, Battersea, London S.W.11.

Christian Action; directors Colin Hodgett, and Nick Beacock; 104 Newgate Street, E.C.1.

Children: Where we going to sleep tonight Mum?
Cathy: ...
Children: Mum, where we going to sleep tonight?
Cathy: ...

from '*Cathy Come Home*'

NEL BESTSELLERS

Crime

T013 332	CLOUDS OF WITNESS	Dorothy L. Sayers	40p
W002 871	THE UNPLEASANTNESS AT THE BELLONA CLUB	Dorothy L. Sayers	30p
W003 011	GAUDY NIGHT	Dorothy L. Sayers	30p
T010 457	THE NINE TAILORS	Dorothy L. Sayers	35p
T012 484	FIVE RED HERRINGS	Dorothy L. Sayers	40p
T012 492	UNNATURAL DEATH	Dorothy L. Sayers	40p

Fiction

W002 775	HATTER'S CASTLE	A. J. Cronin	60p
W002 777	THE STARS LOOK DOWN	A. J. Cronin	60p
T010 414	THE CITADEL	A. J. Cronin	60p
T010 422	THE KEYS OF THE KINGDOM	A. J. Cronin	50p
T001 288	THE TROUBLE WITH LAZY ETHEL	Ernest K. Gann	30p
T003 922	IN THE COMPANY OF EAGLES	Ernest K. Gann	30p
W002 145	THE NINTH DIRECTIVE	Adam Hall	25p
T012 271	THE WARSAW DOCUMENT	Adam Hall	40p
T011 305	THE STRIKER PORTFOLIO	Adam Hall	30p
T007 243	SYLVIA SCARLETT	Compton Mackenzie	30p
T007 669	SYLVIA AND ARTHUR	Compton Mackenzie	30p
T007 677	SYLVIA AND MICHAEL	Compton Mackenzie	35p
W002 772	TO THE CORAL STRAND	John Masters	40p
W002 788	TRIAL AT MONOMOY	John Masters	40p
T009 084	SIR, YOU BASTARD	G. F. Newman	30p
T012 522	THURSDAY MY LOVE	Robert H. Rimmer	40p
T009 769	THE HARRAD EXPERIMENT	Robert H. Rimmer	40p
T010 252	THE REBELLION OF YALE MARRATT	Robert H. Rimmer	40p
T010 716	THE ZOLOTOV AFFAIR	Robert H. Rimmer	30p
T013 820	THE DREAM MERCHANTS	Harold Robbins	75p
W002 783	79 PARK AVENUE	Harold Robbins	50p
T012 255	THE CARPETBAGGERS	Harold Robbins	80p
T011 801	WHERE LOVE HAS GONE	Harold Robbins	70p
T013 707	THE ADVENTURERS	Harold Robbins	80p
T006 743	THE INHERITORS	Harold Robbins	60p
T009 467	STILETTO	Harold Robbins	30p
T010 406	NEVER LEAVE ME	Harold Robbins	30p
T011 771	NEVER LOVE A STRANGER	Harold Robbins	70p
T011 798	A STONE FOR DANNY FISHER	Harold Robbins	60p
T011 461	THE BETSY	Harold Robbins	75p
T010 201	RICH MAN, POOR MAN	Irwin Shaw	80p
W002 186	THE PLOT	Irving Wallace	75p
W002 761	THE SEVEN MINUTES	Irving Wallace	75p
T009 718	THE THREE SIRENS	Irving Wallace	75p
T010 341	THE PRIZE	Irving Wallace	80p

Historical

T009 750	THE WARWICK HEIRESS	Margaret Abbey	30p
T011 607	THE SON OF YORK	Margaret Abbey	30p
T011 585	THE ROSE IN SPRING	Eleanor Fairburn	30p
T009 734	RICHMOND AND ELIZABETH	Brenda Honeyman	30p
T011 593	HARRY THE KING	Brenda Honeyman	35p
T009 742	THE ROSE BOTH RED AND WHITE	Betty King	30p
W002 479	AN ODOUR OF SANCTITY	Frank Yerby	50p
W002 824	THE FOXES OF HARROW	Frank Yerby	50p
W002 916	BENTON'S ROW	Frank Yerby	40p
W003 010	THE VIXENS	Frank Yerby	40p
T006 921	JARRETT'S JADE	Frank Yerby	40p
T010 988	BRIDE OF LIBERTY	Frank Yerby	30p

Science Fiction

T007 081	THE CANOPY OF TIME	Brian Aldiss	30p
W003 003	CARSON OF VENUS	Edgar Rice Burroughs	30p
W002 449	THE MOON IS A HARSH MISTRESS	Robert Heinlein	40p
W002 697	THE WORLDS OF ROBERT HEINLEIN	Robert Heinlein	25p
W002 839	SPACE FAMILY STONE	Robert Heinlein	30p
W002 844	STRANGER IN A STRANGE LAND	Robert Heinlein	60p

T006 778	ASSIGNMENT IN ETERNITY	Robert Heinlein 25p
T007 294	HAVE SPACESUIT – WILL TRAVEL	Robert Heinlein 30p
T009 696	GLORY ROAD	Robert Heinlein 40p
T011 844	DUNE	Frank Herbert 75p
T012 298	DUNE MESSIAH	Frank Herbert 40p
W002 814	THE WORLDS OF FRANK HERBERT	Frank Herbert 30p
W002 911	SANTAROGA BARRIER	Frank Herbert 30p
W003 001	DRAGON IN THE SEA	Frank Herbert 30p

War

W002 921	WOLF PACK	William Hardy 30p
W002 484	THE FLEET THAT HAD TO DIE	Richard Hough 25p
W002 805	HUNTING OF FORCE Z	Richard Hough 30p
W002 632	THE BASTARD BRIGADE	Peter Leslie 25p
T006 999	KILLER CORPS	Peter Leslie 25p
T011 755	TRAWLERS GO TO WAR	Lund and Ludlam 40p
W005 051	GOERING	Manvell & Freankel 52½p
W005 065	HIMMLER	Manvell & Freankel 52½p
W002 423	STRIKE FROM THE SKY	Alexander McKee 30p
W002 831	NIGHT	Francis Pollini 40p
T010 074	THE GREEN BERET	Hilary St. George Saunders 40p
T010 066	THE RED BERET	Hilary St. George Saunders 40p

Western

T010 619	EDGE – THE LONER	George Gilman 25p
T010 600	EDGE – TEN THOUSAND DOLLARS AMERICAN	George Gilman 25p
T010 929	EDGE – APACHE DEATH	George Gilman 25p

General

T011 763	SEX MANNERS FOR MEN	Robert Chartham 30p
W002 531	SEX MANNERS FOR ADVANCED LOVERS	Robert Chartham 25p
W002 835	SEX AND THE OVER FORTIES	Robert Chartham 30p
T010 732	THE SENSUOUS COUPLE	Dr. C. 25p
P002 367	AN ABZ OF LOVE	Inge and Sten Hegeler 60p
P011 402	A HAPPIER SEX LIFE	Dr. Sha Kokken 70p
W002 584	SEX MANNERS FOR SINGLE GIRLS	Georges Valensin 25p
W002 592	THE FRENCH ART OF SEX MANNERS	Georges Valensin 25p
W002 726	THE POWER TO LOVE	E. W. Hirsch M. D. 47½p

Mad

S003 491	LIKE MAD	30p
S003 494	MAD IN ORBIT	30p
S003 520	THE BEDSIDE MAD	30p
S003 521	THE VOODOO MAD	30p
S003 657	MAD FOR BETTER OR VERSE	30p
S003 716	THE SELF MADE MAD	30p

— — — — — — — — — — — — —

NEL P.O. BOX 11, FALMOUTH, CORNWALL

Please send cheque or postal order. Allow 6p per book to cover postage and packing.

Name..

Address ....

....

Title ....
(SEPTEMBER)